NATIVE AMERICAN BEADWORK

Traditional Beading Techniques for the Modern-Day Beadworker

by

GEORG J. BARTH

Foreword by

BILL HOLM

R. SCHNEIDER, PUBLISHERS

Cover illustration: Umatilla blanket-strip panel (Honnen collection; photograph by Bill Holm).
Chapter title "5 Overlay-Stitch": Plateau cradle (Holm collection; photograph by Bill Holm).
Chapter title "6 Crow-Stitch": Transmontane mirror bag (Honnen collection).
Chapter title "8 Woven Beadwork": Ojibwa bandolier bag (Museum für Völkerkunde, Freiburg, Germany).

R. Schneider, Publishers
312 Linwood Avenue
Stevens Point, WI 54481

Manufactured in the United States of America.

ISBN 0-936984-12-0 paper
ISBN 0-936984-13-9 cloth
Library of Congress Catalog Card Number: 91-60320

CONTENTS

FOREWORD

One of the jobs of a museum curator is to talk to all kinds of people who come to the museum for information. Most curators who are deeply involved in the subject of their expertise enjoy this interplay, especially if the inquiries are serious and show that the visitor has "done his homework." In the fall of 1981 a colleague at the University of Washington, a professor of Germanics, brought to my office in the Burke Museum a German couple who had stopped by in Seattle on the way home from a trip to Alaska and who asked to be introduced to me. It was immediately apparent that Georg and Christa Barth were seriously interested in the arts and cultures of Native North America, especially of the Crow and Plateau peoples, and that Georg was not an ordinary hobbyist in his understanding of techniques and styles. Later Georg sent me pictures of himself and his wife impeccably dressed in classic Crow apparel of their own making. I was very impressed and looked forward to hearing more from him.

A few years later I received a letter from Georg in which he commented insightfully on a paper of mine, "Crow-Plateau Beadword: an Effort Toward a Uniform Terminology," published in *Crow Indian Art*. This began a continuing correspondence between us, and an exchange of ideas on the technology and styles of Crow and Plateau art. On one of his visits to Seattle Georg brought me a copy of his book on beadwork techniques, *Techniken der Indianischen Perlenstickerei*. The importance of this work shone through even my faulty German, aided immensely by its clear, accurate, illustrations. I showed my copy to several expert beadworker friends, who immediately wanted copies of their own, in spite of the fact that they read no German at all! Georg had told me that he hoped to publish a translation or, more accurately, a version written in English, an idea that was greeted with enthusiasm by those who had seen the German edition. Over the next few years I had the opportunity to read and comment on the manuscript of the English version as it progressed, and I came to believe even more strongly that this was to be the most complete and thorough treatment of the subject of traditional Indian beadwork techniques yet to be seen. My own experience over the years as a researcher, teacher, and craftsman has led me to believe that there is no better way to acquire understanding of an art tradition than to have a hands-on experience with the reproduction of the products of that tradition. Georg Barth's work is the proof of that idea. He is untiring in his pursuit of complete understanding of each technique he tackles. And he is able to translate that understanding to the printed page.

Now we have Georg's book! It is a product of a combination of deep admiration for the beadwork of Native North America, and Georg's German *gründlichkeit* (thoroughness, to which Georg admits!). One has only to look at the drawings and diagrams, many of them new to the English edition and others redrawn to increase their clarity, to see just how thorough he has been. These are without any doubt the best diagrams of techniques to be seen in print. It is not a simple matter to reduce the movements of needle, thread, and strings of beads to clear, understandable, line drawings, but Georg Barth has done it! Among the most innovative are his gourd and Comanche-stitch diagrams, redone for the English edition to show the beadwork encircling the foundation. He even includes realistic graph paper pages for several variations on those cylindrical beading techniques, as well as graph sheets for lane-stitch and woven beadwork (with spaces realistically left for the warp threads!). Georg's interest in the mathematical basis for Indian aesthetics, especially in peyote beadwork, is expressed in formulas designed to assist those of similar interest. For those of us with fewer mathematical skills, he has thoughtfully provided a handy table with the calculations done for us.

8

In addition to those impressive drawings, there are photographs of fine examples of the various techniques, which set standards of appearance for beadworkers using the book. Some of these photographs are of Georg's own work, and should serve as an inspiration to those who aspire to make fine beadwork.

Georg Barth's book will make you want to bead if you haven't done so, and to improve and expand your techniques if you have. Now just where did I put my beeswax?

Bill Holm, Curator Emeritus
Thomas Burke Memorial Washington State Museum
University of Washington

PREFACE

I vividly remember a Sunday morning in February 1959—I was a 12-year-old boy then—when I browsed through the pages of a youth magazine. Suddenly I was stopped by an article which gave detailed instructions on how to make an authentic feather bonnet. To any kid, such a bonnet purely and simply symbolized the American Indian, and from that very moment on I was hopelessly in love with anything that had to do with American Indian art and culture. A couple of years later, for the first time I saw authentic Indian apparel in the Linden-Museum in Stuttgart, and I was immediately attracted to the flamboyant colors and bold designs of the Crow horse trappings displayed in the glass cases.

More and more I became intrigued by the beauty and harmony found in Indian beadwork in general and classic Crow-style beadwork in particular. It was soon apparent that in order to get a better understanding of this unique art form, I had to research it. But books and visits to other museum and private collections did not tell the whole truth. Only through the experience of beading for many, many hours, I learned to understand the interplay of techniques, designs, colors, and dimensions in the Crow beading style; only then I was able to compose my own beadwork ornaments and yet stay within the conventions of the style.

Over the years, the insights gained from beading many articles made me expand my research to other techniques not related to Crow beadwork. One of the most important and most fascinating observations was the give-and-take between technique and style. To understand style I had to acquire an intimate knowledge of technique; whenever learning a new one I've made it a habit to ask myself what was going on and why this technique was done that way. On the other hand, by researching unfamiliar beading techniques, such as bead weaving or the various gourd-stitch methods, I learned a lot more about the beaded art of tribes that had not caught my attention as much as Crow beadwork did.

I am most interested in Native American *textile* arts—particularly in techniques which cannot be reproduced by machines, such as beadwork, quillwork, basketry, or the twining of Chilkat dancing blankets. That this was to become the keynote of my research, I realized when I began collecting cornhusk bags and basket hats of the Plateau tribes. Learning how these things were made and how to reproduce them faithfully leaves me in awe of, and with deep respect for the American Indian artists and craftspeople who created them.

During the 1890s, when Buffalo Bill's Wild West Show traveled the European continent, many German visitors became so intrigued that they were motivated to form "Cowboy and Indian clubs" where they tried to emulate Indian life style (BOLZ K 1987:480–484). This surprisingly widespread appreciation has never waned over the decades; in various European countries, people of all ages and professions continue to be interested in the history and culture of the American Indians. Imagine a hike through some German countryside on Pentecost weekend: you wouldn't believe your eyes if you suddenly saw a huge circle of tipis, with hundreds of people clad in buckskin, feathers, and beads. Only when you take a closer look at their pale complexions and hear Bavarian, Saxon, and other German dialects, you will be reminded that you are not out on the Plains in Sitting Bull's camp.

While visiting a few of these powwows and talking with many hobbyists, I became aware of the lack of good German publications on Indian beadwork. So I decided to make my experiences of many years of beading available to a wider public and wrote *Techniken der Indianischen Perlenstickerei*. Instead of merely drawing on the literature already existing, I felt strongly that I should analyze all beading techniques that I knew of, not only in practice but also in theory. I wanted to learn about their strengths and weaknesses and, most important, to find out how to teach these beading techniques in a way easy to understand. When my American publisher and I discussed an English translation, it soon became clear that I would need to revise my German book completely and write a new and expanded English version.

Because of my own focus on 19th century Plains and Plateau Indian beadwork, this book's emphasis inevitably is on old-time beadwork and reproducing this kind of beadwork. Although I have tried to present the beading techniques in their cultural context, I have felt that, as long as the appearance of the finished beadwork is not affected, some minor concessions to the modern-day bead-worker should be made—such as the use of cotton-thread instead of sinew. But while working on the book I became more and more aware of Indian beadwork being a strong and living tradition among Native Americans.

As an art lover I appreciate a piece of art the way I see it at the moment I see it. Thus, despite the repeated references to the historic use of various beading techniques, this book has no intention to be an historical analysis of Native American beadwork or its development through the times.

Nor can it be an analysis of beading styles. *Technique* is a physical process and can be fairly easily broken down into its individual elements; it can by analyzed step by step, and once understood, it can be reproduced. *Style*, however, depends on many factors which are not as easily pinned down or even explained: tradition, society, art, religion, economic conditions, environment, as well as influences from foreign cultures; all of which may play important roles in evaluating and understanding a given style (CONN *B* 1960).

Taste, harmony, and elegance—time and again I observe these most characteristic features whenever I see a fine piece of Indian beadwork. No matter which tribe made it or what time it was beaded, each one is a masterpiece. It has been said that there is no word in Indian languages which would translate precisely our word "tradition." But they have ways to express exactly the same meaning: "Doing things the right way" (COE *I* 1986:46).

With many fine books and articles available on the history and tribal styles of American Indian art, the bibliography at the end of this book will help you to find additional interesting literature pertaining to the many aspects of Native American beadwork. To organize the entries under subject headings rather than just list them alphabetically, I had to add a letter to the bibliographic references in the running text: "(LOEB *F* 1980:45)" for example, means that in the bibliography this title is found in section "F" ("Transmontane Style [Crow & Plateau]").

Despite the rare moments when I asked myself why I stay involved with this project over several years, writing this book was an important experience which I will never want to miss because I learned so much myself about Native American beadwork. And looking back is a good moment to say "Thank you."

In the very first place, my thanks must go to Bill Holm who, unknowingly and long before we met personally, has very much influenced my approach to American Indian art. His classic *Northwest Coast Indian Art: An Analysis of Form* was a real breakthrough in my own research of classic Crow-style beadwork—transposing his precise methodology to Intermontane beaded art helped me to single out and organize its elements, and to understand their functions and relationships much better. I take the greatest pleasure in thanking him for his steady encouragement, for reading the manuscript, adding many invaluable comments and discussing various important issues, and for writing the Foreword. A number of objects from his collection help to illustrate the techniques discussed in the book. Knowing that we share many ideas about Native American art and its research has always been one of the most important stimuli for my own work. Above all, I will always remember his help which was more than generous.

Steve Honnen has opened doors in my mind to view beadwork in general, and Transmontane beadwork in particular, in a wider context, to perceive it as art in its purest sense, the utilitarian function of the objects thus decorated notwithstanding. Throughout the years, he has supported my Crow beadwork research as well as my work on this book. I love to recall the hospitality which I enjoyed at his home when we sat together and discussed Transmontane beadwork, pointing to many interesting details and enjoying its beauty. Many fine pieces of Transmontane beadwork in his collection illustrate this book.

Thanks for permissions to reproduce objects from their collections go to: Thomas Burke Memorial Washington State Museum (Seattle, Washington); Wisconsin State Historical Society (Madison, Wisconsin); Museum für Völkerkunde (Berlin, Germany); Museum für Völkerkunde (Freiburg, Germany); and Linden-Museum (Stuttgart, Germany).

Peter Bolz (Berlin, Germany) was so kind to verify a special technique used in diagonal weaving; Ian M. West (Horsted Keynes, England) generously permitted me to photograph his collection and read several chapters; Rex Reddick, (Denison, Texas) read the chapter on Gourd-Stitch and provided useful comments; F. Dennis Lessard's (Santa Fe, New Mexico) comments on Woven Beadwork made me completely revise parts of this chapter.

Thanks to Alice Scherer, director of the Center for the Study of Beadwork in Portland/Oregon for her encouraging words. When I met her and many other bead(work) enthusiasts during the Bead Conference in Santa Fe in March 1992, I became aware of a widespread interest in beadwork of all kinds which has been unknown to me before.

My publisher, Richard Schneider, even went to the trouble to come over from the States to discuss details of the book. Not minding the jet-lag, he immediately plunged into the work of revising the many pages of my manuscript and discussing many details of layout and format. This visit was followed by a continuous and lively correspondence, and his numerous invaluable comments and criticisms on language and style tremendously helped to shape my text into good American English and added many subtleties to my vocabulary. Above all I have to thank him for his patience and faith in my work.

For her support and patience, I have to offer my deepest gratitude to my wife, Christa. Probably her most important advice was "Stop rewriting," and without her help and unflagging faith throughout the years, this book would never have been possible.

1
BEADS

Murano, a little island near Venice, Italy, has been for many centuries the major center of glass manufacture, and still today you can visit a few furnaces and watch the glass blowers at their work, although bead production has become less and less important. Over the centuries, thousands of tons of beads were exported to America and Africa, and as late as the early 1960's various trading posts still offered many beautiful Italian old-time bead colors for sale.

Throughout the centuries the Venetian bead manufacturers took any measure to keep the ingredients of their melts secret, and for some time glass workers trying to defect with the formulas had to face capital punishment; if they succeeded, their relatives were imprisoned to induce the emigrants' return. Although these severe regulations helped the doges of Venice to establish a powerful position in the market or almost monopolize it, they could not prevent the rise of bead manufacturing centers in other parts of Europe. With the old knowledge long gone, the few bead makers today are rarely successful in reproducing the original nuances found in museum pieces. Unlike the larger and more spectacular polychrome "trade beads," seed beads have never been given special attention, and they remain an important area still untapped by in-depth research.

To a lesser degree, beads were also imported from France and Holland, but in the late 19th century seed beads from Bohemia (then part of the Austrian Empire and now of Czechoslovakia) began to dominate the market. The Venetian beads have been known for their soft and subdued colors that blended perfectly with the tasteful designs found in the tribal styles. The brighter colors of the new Czech beads often tend toward a bluish tint, which, in most cases may not be noticeable, but will strike the beholder immediately when seen on replicas of articles that originally used Italian colors.

The new colors and particularly the uniform shape of the Czech beads appealed to the Indian beadworkers, so sales of Italian beads dwindled more and more. Today it is not unusual to pay twenty or thirty dollars for one ounce of the old Italian seed bead colors, so you would take care not to spill any of them! As a matter of fact, "bead hunting" has become a hobby of its own for the connoisseur beadworker.

Craftworkers, who are primarily interested in creating authentic replicas of old-time Indian clothing and accoutrements, may deplore the present situation, while modern Indian beadworkers enjoy a wide selection of bright-colored Czech beads. So if you're in for modern style beadwork—which I have always admired for its excellent craftsmanship and colorful designs—you needn't pay strict attention to most of what I will have to say about shapes and colors used in old-time beadwork.

BEAD SIZES

As with so many things in everyday life, bead sizes have been standardized, too: "10/o" up to "20/o" for *seed* beads, and "6/o" to "9/o" for *pony* beads (Fig. 1-1). In some books or articles you will see these sizes written as "10°" which means the same as "10/o." Some authors writing about Indian beadwork use Italian sizes, with the most common "4/o" and "5/o" equaling roughly 12/o and 13/o respectively. They are not exactly the same, however!

To most beadworkers these numbers have always been enigmatic, so we have put up with the fact that small beads are classified by large numbers, and larger ones, like the pony beads, by small numbers, or, in other words, the number is reciprocal to the size of the bead. The rationale behind this "mystery," though, is simple: the number before the slash denotes the number of bead *rows* of a given size there are to an inch; thus *thirteen* rows beaded in size "13/o" will roughly cover one inch (2.54 cm) (Fig. 1-2). Although this bit of information should not be taken as an absolute one, it is very helpful in judging the area size a design

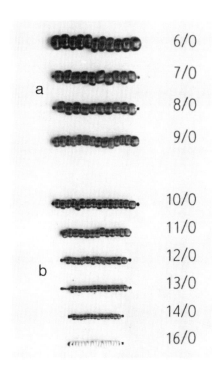

a

6/0

7/0

8/0

9/0

b

10/0

11/0

12/0

13/0

14/0

16/0

Fig. 1-1. *Bead chart showing actual bead sizes.*

Among the pony bead sizes 6/o to 9/o shown here, size 8/o beads probably were those most commonly used size in old-time pony beadwork.
Seed bead sizes 12/o to 14/o were the most favored bead sizes in old-time beadwork while it is not unusual to observe still smaller beads (size 16/o) on some pieces. The beadworkers of the Crow or Nez Perce often used 10/o beads for edging cloth-trims.

will cover as well as determining the bead size(s) used when researching old beadwork (BUGELSKI *B* 1989: 37).

Beads of the sizes 12/o or 13/o were most commonly used in old-time seed beadwork, and it is not unusual to find 14/o or 16/o beads on many old pieces; almost unbelievably, even tiny 18/o or 20/o beads were used to make the finest beadwork ever seen (CONN *I* 1985:76). In Oklahoma, 13/o or 14/o seem to be the preferred sizes for gourd-stitch or peyote beadwork, while Sioux men on the Rosebud Reservation in South Dakota have been known to buy completed fans for the feathers, only to discard the beadwork and replace it by the favored 16/o beads (LESSARD *D* 1984:24).

Pony beads of size 8/o or 9/o, most popular in the early era of Indian beadwork, were still used in the classic period for wide undulating lanes on Blackfeet or Plateau women's dresses. The Crow beadworkers favored these large beads for edging some of their cloth-bound articles, while in the Columbia Plateau region, pony beadwork, combined with seed beads, was continued until the turn of the century.

It is true that many old-time craftswomen among the various tribes added variety to their beadwork by using different bead sizes in a single piece. Crow-style beadwork, again, is a classic example of this common practice, which in some cases, might have been dictated by a shortage of beads, but more often was done by choice. On a Transmontane-style blanket-strip panel you may often notice some of the design elements beaded with 13/o seed beads, while others are done with 8/o pony beads (Fig. 1-2). However, if you take another look, you will notice that each of these fields forms an individually worked unit; almost never will you find beads of different sizes between the two ends of a single row. Because overlaid floral designs usually are worked as individual units, they may be beaded with a size differing from that of the neighboring area.

Fig. 1-2. *13 rows of 13/o seed beads cover a width of roughly one inch, while it takes 8 rows of 8/o pony beads to cover an inch (Beadwork by the author).*

In geometric overlay- or lane-stitch beadwork, the same bead size was maintained throughout the length of a row, and only in lane-stitch (or Crow-stitch) pieces using simple block-designs may you see a 13/o row next to a 11/o or even pony bead row. Because both rows are laid out straight, they do not affect each other's course, as would rows with differently-sized beads.

A myth, cropping up time and again in "how-to" books, should be dispelled: beading with small 13/o beads is *no* more difficult than with size 10/o or even pony beads! If you are a beginner to Indian beadwork, I urge you not to heed any advice to use larger beads: you will have a hard time to kick a bad habit. And if you think that pony beads with their large holes must be still easier to handle, the contrary is true. You will experience this when you try to do Crow-stitch or overlay-stitch beadwork with pony beads: the thread (or sinew) carrying the beads is not as close to the backing material as with seed beads, and the second thread sewing down the beads is likely to pull down the bead thread and cause dips in the bead row (CONN *A* 1972:12). Of course, if you are going to emulate beadwork of the early fur trade era, you *must* work with pony beads, and you *must* learn how to bead correctly with them.

BEAD SHAPES

Most old beads were rather narrow; i.e., the diameter was significantly larger than the thickness, and a few colors sometimes may even be shaped like tiny rings. Some modern reproductions of the old-colored beads match the original colors pretty closely, but very seldom do they also have the right shape. For ten years I had searched for the correct shade of light blue found in most classic Crow beadwork. When I finally found it, I had to accept the barrel shape of the beads, which is a typical trait of these reproductions (Fig. 1-3). Narrow beads are much better suited to smooth overlay work than the barrel-shaped ones. If you want to learn more about the shapes as well as the colors used by the old-time beadworkers, consult *The Blackfeet: Artists of the Northern Plains* (SCRIVER *D* 1990) which contains many magnificent close-up photographs of Blackfeet beadwork.

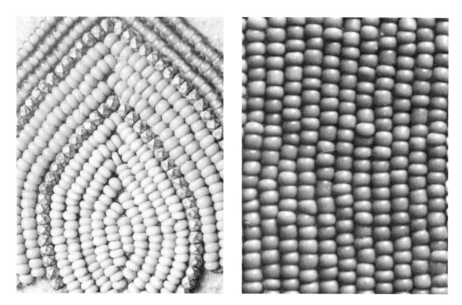

Fig. 1-3. *Old-time beads compared with new reproductions. Left: Rather narrow beads on a Blackfeet moccasin (Author's collection). Right: Modern Italian or French reproductions of old-time beads often have a squarish shape.*

While reproductions of old-time beads are sold in small bags, most Czech beads can be bought on *hanks*; beads are strung on thin thread loops about 20 in. (50 cm) long, and usually 10 to 12 loops make a hank, weighing roughly one ounce or 30 grams. Although this aspect may seem trivial, beads on strings can be more easily examined for size and uniformity by wrapping a couple of loops around your index finger for critical inspection.

In Native American beadwork, and more so today in gourd-stitched peyote beadwork, Czech cut beads have always been popular. Adding an extra charm because of their facetted surfaces, they flash or sparkle in the light. Short, tubular *basket beads* with uneven edges were very common on the Northern Plains and the Columbia Plateau and used for decorating dress yokes; unfortunately, these beads are no longer available.

During the Reservation period in the late 19th century, tubular beads, often called *bugle beads*, were widely used by the Blackfeet women to decorate the yokes of their cloth dresses.

BEAD COLORS

We can only be envious of the wide palette of colors the 19th century Indian beadworkers could choose from—on some of the old sample charts I observed almost eighty different hues and nuances of colors. The wide spectrum of colors available is reflected in the old beadwork to such a degree that I might go out on a limb if I tried to present hard and fast rules for the correct usage of colors. Only continuous research in museums will provide you with an intimate knowledge of old-time bead colors.

Describing colors in words only is an almost impossible task; nonetheless and despite the sad fact that most of these colors will never again be available, I will try to present a brief outline of the most significant and most-used old-time bead colors, without claiming it to be a complete one.

WHITE.   Chalk-white beads were most commonly used in old-time beadwork, while frequently bluish, slightly translucent milk-white beads, as well as clear glass beads without any tint can be observed on many old objects.

YELLOW.   A classic color was the so-called "greasy yellow," a dull, translucent yellow tone which can be found in various shades. However, clear transparent yellow, opaque corn-yellow, and pumpkin-orange, were also widely used.

PINK.   Next to light blue, pink or "old rose," often called "Cheyenne pink," was one of the most popular colors in Northern Plains, Crow, and Plateau beadwork—so dominant in fact, that it became a characteristic feature of these styles. As a rule, these pinks featured a purplish tint, while lavender, another favorite shade which actually is a purple with a pink overtone, added a cool elegance to that type of beadwork.

"ROSE-WHITE-INSIDE."   One cf the most striking colors, found throughout all tribes doing beadwork, was a transparent red- or rose-tone with a white core, known as "rose-white-inside," "underwhite," or "Cornaline d'Aleppo." Most frequently a rich, ruby red,

occasionally with a barely noticeable bluish or brownish touch, was available to the beadworkers.

Authentic colors being extremely difficult to recreate , most of the recent reproductions are either too pale—almost like a weak pink—or, more often, they turn out as bright red, or brick red shades. As a matter of fact, these are *not* the real thing and most likely will ruin any attempt at a faithful duplication of old-time beadwork. No matter how sparingly this color may have been used, it governed the appearance of any beaded piece.

RED. In more recent times, transparent red and purple were used. On the Southern Plains, the old-time beadworkers favored a deep, transparent, burgundy red, which together with a dark powder blue created a distinct color scheme. Modern beadwork, on the other hand, being so different in style, design and colors, combines very well with the bright Czech red.

BLUE. Blue beads were among the first colors the Indians encountered, and their predilection for this color has remained to the present day. The spectrum of blue tones ranged from chalk blue (light ultramarine blue), a washed-out turquoise blue or gray blue, light and darker shades of turquoise blues, through the middle ranges of bright royal blue and powder blue, all the way to dark royal blue, navy blue, and an almost black midnight blue, with the dark shades also appearing in transparent versions.

GREEN. The most important and commonly-used green colors should be mentioned: light green or apple green, quite popular in later classic Sioux beadwork; a medium green or "Crow green;" transparent bluish bottle green of a medium shade; and opaque as well as transparent dark greens.

BLACK. During the peak of seed beadwork, black lost its importance; however, it was still used, for example, in the sacred beadwork of the Cheyenne. The Middle West and the Plateau tribes still used black beads to a great deal; pony-beaded dresses of the Blackfeet often feature black bands, usually separated by white bands or lanes.

METALLIC. Facetted brass, steel, and iron beads were prized around the turn of the century on the Plains. Having been the fashion of a short period, metallic beads may be used for dating certain pieces more precisely (GALLAGHER, POWELL C 1953). Among the northern Athapaskan beadworkers, metallic beads of both the silver and gold tones have been popular until today, displaying even regional preferences (DUNCAN H 1989:66).

ANALYZING OLD PHOTOGRAPHS. Because color photography started only in this century, we often have to resort to old black-and-white photographs to find design suggestions for our own beadwork. Assuming some familiarity with a particular beading style and its colors, you may be able to interpret the tonal values in the design elements depicted. However, you should always bear in mind that the negative plates used in 19th century photography, as well as the early orthochromatic films, were most sensitive to the hues in the blue range, rendering them very light, while parts

 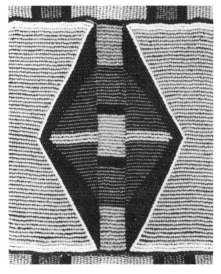

Fig. 1-4. *Rendition of colors and tonal values in different black-and-white films, showing the blanket-strip panel on the cover. Left: Orthochromatic film which distorts the tonal values. Right: Panchromatic film which shows the true tonal values (Honnen collection, photographs by Bill Holm).*

beaded yellow turned out very dark and red beads almost black (Fig. 1-4, left). Only when panchromatic films became available was true rendition of tonal values possible (HOLM *B* 1985).

RUNNING OUT OF COLORS.   Especially when you are beading large background areas you may run out of the color—a situation any old-time Indian beadworker probably was confronted with more than once. She would either use beads of a similar shade, or try to buy new beads during her next visit to the agency store or the trading post; still, she would not be sure to get the same shades. As a beadworker making replicas, I have grown fond of these color breaks. Sometimes I put them in deliberately, paying attention to a logical sequence of shade variation. Some of the color-breaks, however, appear quite arbitrary, and the beadworker might have known well ahead that she will run out of that specific color. Again, modern taste may not tolerate color breaks, so you'd be well advised to buy enough beads before starting beading a larger piece.

HANDLING YOUR BEADS

STORING THE BEADS.   Having put considerable efforts into collecting good colors and different sizes of beads—often expensive and hard to come by, especially when you plan to make reproductions of old-style beadwork—they should be stored carefully. As I have bought most of my beads in loose bulks I have made it a habit to store them in jelly or honey jars which can be found in most households; their lids provide ideal containers for pouring in the beads into while doing beadwork; pouring the beads of various colors on a piece of cloth to select from, as is suggested by some authors, should be strongly discouraged as the beads certainly will become mixed sooner or later. A funnel helps pouring back the beads into the jars without spilling them.

SCOOPING THE BEADS.   Running the needle through the beads in the lid several times in a scooping motion is a fast way to collect enough beads and a method which I have used whenever doing sewn beadwork. Three to four rapid "scoops" usually fill the needle to the tip. Inspect the beads gathered on the needle for size and uniformity and change oddly-shaped beads that might disturb the smooth surface of the finished work. When doing lane-stitch work, count the beads necessary for the row or design section and remove the surplus beads. For overlay-stitch or Crow-stitch work, the length needed is simply measured and filled up with beads. Checking them on the thread before sewing down saves a lot of frustration: if an offending bead should be discovered in the middle of a long row, it is easier to break it with an awl or pliers rather than to remove all beads from the thread.

TAKING BEADS FROM HANKS. As was mentioned earlier in this chapter, most if not all Italian seed beads were available on hanks (modern Czech beads are still sold on hanks), and very likely were taken directly from them on the needle or sinew tip; thus the scooping technique became only necessary when most of the old bead colors became available only in loose bulk form during the recent years.

Using this method of gathering beads, you simply cut open one strand of the hank; you need only one pass of the needle to get all the beads of a color on. You will learn quite quickly to accurately judge the number of beads needed when doing lane-stitch beadwork, without actually counting the individual beads. Even if you have loose beads only and still prefer to string them "from the hank," you may want to use a "spinning wheel" to string all loose beads on a thread before taking the beads from it. Such spinning wheels can be bought from some bead suppliers—follow the instructions that come with this tool.

Great Lakes-style loomwork with its elaborate designs, and gourd-stitch work, of course, are not suited to either method of stringing beads, as these techniques require taking up single beads to create patterns. This also applies to edge-beading which rarely uses more than three or four beads in a single stitch.

2
MATERIALS

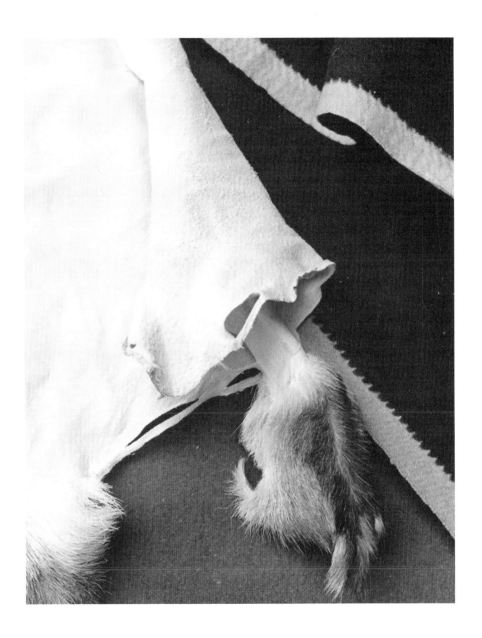

No matter if you plan a small strike-a-light bag in the Kiowa style or a fully-beaded Cheyenne cradle cover, the same amount of attention has to be paid to the selection of the right kind of hide or leather, let alone the proper use of designs and their careful arrangement on the object. The amount of time and effort you put into the preparation of a beadwork project should ideally equal that of the actual beading itself.

Beads were sewn on soft materials such as brain-tanned hides, woolen cloth, and canvas, or on stiff materials such as rawhide, or harness leather which was obtained from White traders. While the native materials had been used for generations, the Indian beadworkers quickly saw the potentials of fabrics and commercial leather and adapted their methods to the new materials whenever they felt like using them.

SOFT-TANNED HIDES OR BUCKSKIN

As I mentioned before, most beadwork was done on the brain-tanned and smoked hides of bighorn sheep, pronghorn antelope, deer, elk, moose, and bison, to name the most important animals. When game became scarce in the Reservation times, the craftswomen of the Sioux, as well as other tribes, even beaded on cow hides. To make your beading efforts enjoyable, your leather or buckskin should meet at least the following requirements: (1) it should be soft enough for a needle to pass through without having to prepunch holes with an awl; (2) at the same time it should be firm enough to support your beadwork; (3) if possible, it should be sueded on both sides.

Your first and best choice, however, for any kind of Indian-style beadwork and for authentic reproductions of old-time beadwork in particular should be real *brain-tanned* leather of deer, bighorn, elk, moose, or antelope. No matter if smoked or in its natural off-white, it is a beautiful material and once you have felt it with your hands and beaded on it, you probably would never want to work with any other kind of buckskin again! Brain-tanned leather simply cannot be surpassed by even the best substitute. If you can afford them, you may purchase ready-tanned hides from tanners advertising in various magazines, or you may want to learn brain-tanning your own hides, following any of the instructions which have been published elsewhere (BELITZ *K* 1973, HEINBUCH *K* 1990:77–85, MCPHERSON *K* 1986, SCHNEIDER *B* 1972:66–83).

PIECING LEATHER SCRAPS. Larger panels which are to be beaded completely can be pieced together from leather scraps with a fine overcast-stitch since the seams will be covered by the beadwork; in fact, this was a traditional method on the reservations when the women had to salvage the smallest scraps (KANT *D* 1989:68). Articles no longer used often were recycled and turned into new, different items.

 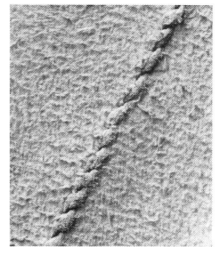

Fig. 2-1. *Front and back view of a smooth seam, featuring the typical undulations between the almost invisible stitches.*

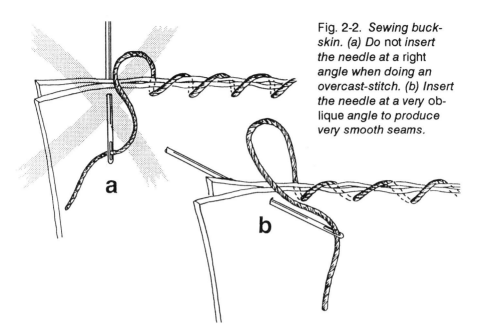

Fig. 2-2. *Sewing buck-skin. (a) Do* not *insert the needle at a* right angle *when doing an overcast-stitch. (b) Insert the needle at a very* oblique *angle to produce very smooth seams.*

Inserting the needle at an *oblique* angle (Fig. 2-2b) very likely may be the secret of the seams which I observed on many old pieces. As a result, the oblique stitches will expose only a tiny bit of thread on the right side of the seam and they help to pronounce the undulations typical for these seams (Fig. 2-1), adding a decorative touch. When the seam is finished, briskly pull out the two parts several times with both hands; a well-done seam will stand this rough treatment without breaking the thread or tearing the leather. With the dull edge of scissors or with your thumb-nail run several times over the inside of the seam to flatten it additionally.

RAWHIDE AND COMMERCIAL LEATHER

The Crow and the Plateau tribes made a number of articles with beads sewn right on the rawhide, among them keyhole-shaped forehead ornaments decorated with horsehair tassels , which were tied to rawhide bridles, or knife sheaths which were often painted with a glossy red. Stiff, medium to dark brown "commercial leather," salvaged from harnesses and stock saddles, or often

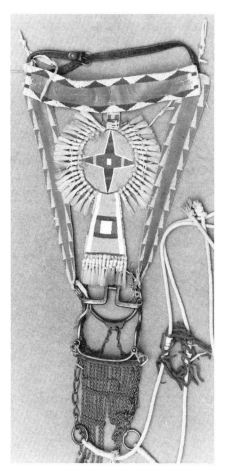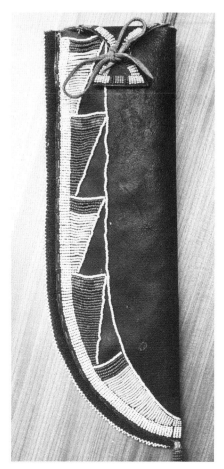

Fig. 2-3. *Beadwork on rawhide. Left: Crow "keyhole" ornament and bridle (Honnen collection; photograph by Bill Holm). Right: Crow-style knife sheath with beads and red paint (Beadwork by the author).*

bartered with that purpose in mind, provided many uses for the Indian craftworkers: panel belts, ration ticket pouches, strike-a-light bags, or horse trappings such as the highly decorative cruppers which the Crow women put on their parade horses.

As both rawhide and harness leather are too heavy and stiff to push the needle through, holes have to be pre-punched with an awl: (1) draw the lane lines with a sharp, hard-grade pencil (Fig. 2-4a); (2) always punch the holes in pairs—the first hole of a pair

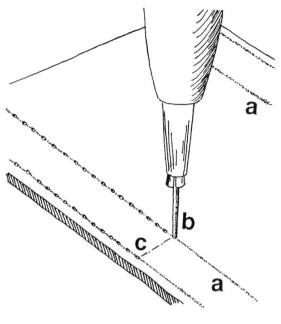

Fig. 2-4. *Pre-punching holes on rawhide and harness leather. (a) Drawing guidelines with pencil. (b & c) Punching pairs of holes on these lines.*

on one line (Fig. 2-4b), then its twin on the other line (Fig. 2-4c). Try to align these pairs of holes carefully and do not forget to place a wooden board under the rawhide or harness leather to protect your work surface.

CANVAS

After most of the indigenous game had been gone—due to over-hunting by Whites and Indians alike, as well as extensive farming and cattle raising—the beadworkers of the Northern Plains and Transmontane region resorted to government-issued canvas for much of their overlay and Crow-stitch beadwork. Using canvas as a beading foundation therefore may be quite authentic, because its stiffness is well-suited to these techniques. Although canvas has today become a widely accepted material to bead on, I still would strongly recommend to use well-tanned buckskin, which, especially if it is smoked, provides you with a much better foundation for beadwork.

WOOLEN CLOTH

Among the tribes of the Upper Great Lakes region, the Northern Plains, the Columbia Plateau, subarctic Canada, and the Northwest Coast, much of the floral beadwork was done on woolen cloth. These fabrics mostly came from England and were traded to the Indians in huge quantities. Also called "stroud cloth" or "strouding" after its alleged source of production in Stroud/Gloucestershire in England, this coarse square- or plain-weave cloth with the characteristic undyed and sawtoothed selvage was very much favored by the Indians for their dress clothing, and the most popular colors were dark navy blue and deep scarlet, while the Plateau people also seemed to have a predilection for green trade cloth.

Black lines woven into the white selvage exemplify a late type of stroud cloth, traded from the Hudson's Bay Company to the Canadian tribes only; this may be a useful feature in identifying tribal or regional origins of native beadwork (FEDER *E* 1968:6). On the Southern Plains, navy and scarlet broadcloth with "rainbow" selvages has been popular with the tribes for a long time.

Among the Crow and the Plateau tribes, trade cloth (primarily the red color) was used to fill in background areas with color (Fig. 2-5); most items using red cloth in the design will use red beads as accents only, or to "tie" the design together. Perhaps the method of cloth inserts stems from the early days when these areas were painted, as on the rectangular neck bibs of shirts. Some scholars think that filling empty spaces with cloth patches, instead of beading a whole cloth panel, was done to save this precious material. Others have argued that "white beads applied over red or blue wool leave hints of background showing through, which would give the white a pale pink or pale blue undertone and the bright red and blue around it" (LOEB *F* 1983:208). My own beading experience as well as original Transmontane beadwork, however, have clearly shown that white lanes beaded on red or blue cloth still show a true white.

I think several reasons made red cloth popular as background fillers: (1) it was easier to bead the designs on *hide* and fill the empty spaces with cloth patches in appliqué fashion; (2) the cloth was available; (3) it had the right tonal value for background

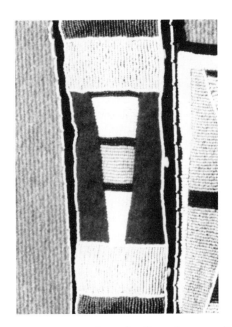

Fig. 2-5. *Left: Part of a Crow horse collar, showing the red cloth inserts around the inverted triangle (Honnen collection; photograph by Bill Holm). Right: Lanes beaded on cloth, as on this Crow-style panel legging (Beadwork by the author).*

purposes; (4) it had a coarse texture similar to bead rows; (5) from an aesthetic point of view, large fields covered with red cloth looked better than beaded with expensive rose-white-inside beads.

THREAD

Almost all old beadwork was done with *sinew* which still today is the best material for sewing beads! Indian beadworkers, of course, had tried commercial linen or cotton threads, but very soon they returned to stringing the beads on sinew. In old lane-stitch bead-work, the bead rows feel as firm as if the beads were strung on wire.

When I started Indian-style beading many years ago, I used polyester or "Nymo" threads because these were recommended by most suppliers and/or authors. Although this type of thread was very strong, I very soon worried about its stretching, which ruined quite a bit of my beadwork. So I decided to use *cotton* thread and have been using this type of thread since then very satisfyingly, no matter how much most authorities on beadwork have advised against using it. Cotton thread, indeed, may wear thin at the needle's eye in the actual sewing process, but usually it does not on the finished article. All my beadwork sewn with well-waxed cotton thread has turned out beautifully, with bead rows almost as firm as if done with sinew, even after a number of years; I wouldn't use any other thread for beading except real sinew!

I strongly recommend *mercerized cotton* of size 50, which usually comes on spools containing a length of 175 yards (160 meters). Doubled size 40 thread fills the bead holes better, but at the same time is more prone to wearing thin in the needle's eye, because of the repeated passing through tiny bead holes or stubborn leather, so you might prefer the finer thread of size 50. White thread is fine, and authentic as well. Brown thread, which is often found on museum pieces, was once white and oxidized to a brownish tint, because of the harsh bleaches used in manufacturing (LAMB C 1983:1), so you wouldn't want to simulate chemical processes. Locating reliable sources for this type of thread in your vicinity may be difficult, so ask your trading post to stock this material and order sufficient quantities.

For *pony bead*work you can use a thicker cotton or linen thread; its size will depend on the needle's eye, as you should always work with the smallest needle possible. However, for sewing down pony bead rows in the overlay- or Crow-stitch method, use well-waxed cotton thread as recommended for seed beadwork.

USING DOUBLED THREAD.   When you do not use sinew you should *always* double the thread you string the beads on, unless noted otherwise (as in loomwork or gourd-stitch beadwork). In other words, threads carrying beads are doubled, while tacking threads needed in the overlay-stitch and Crow-stitch are single only.

The length of your outstretched arm is a good working length for the thread to start with. Of course, to get a doubled strand, you have to pull two arm-lengths from the spool, which makes about

30 in. (75 cm) of doubled thread. This provides you with some beading before you have to take a new thread, as the following example shows: one bead row in lane-stitched Sioux beadwork typically carries nine beads of, let's say, 13/o beads, which makes the row about half an inch (1.2 cm) long—thus your working thread will suffice for roughly 60 to 62 rows, producing almost 4 3/4 in. (12 cm) of a lane. (For the sake of clarity, in most of the illustrations, I have refrained from showing the thread doubled. However, if not stated specifically to the contrary, the bead thread should always be doubled.)

WAXING THE THREAD. To avoid knots and tangles, cotton thread must be completely waxed with *pure beeswax*. It helps to make the thread more durable and reduces the wearing out of the thread as it is repeatedly pulled through the leather: pull the whole length of the thread several times through the wax-cake; it is more important, however, to pull the thread several times between your fingers to really work the wax into the thread. It's not a bad idea to repeat this process during your working session to keep the thread well waxed at any time!

THREADING A NEEDLE. This nightmare of a job, of course, is dreaded by most novice beadworkers with clumsy hands, and even advanced craftspeople find themselves constantly fighting with this problem. I have developed a technique that has worked perfectly with cotton thread—it is a rare moment that I have to try more than once to get the thread even through the finest needle's eye!

(1) *Break*, instead of cut, the required length from the spool—this will result in a frayed end (Fig. 2-6a); (2) pull this *end* (for a length of 2 in. [5 cm]) several times through the wax cake; (3) with your fingertips form this frayed end to a sharp point, with the compressed fibers tapering into a hair-like extension; (4) cut off the "hair" with a pair of small scissors, taking care that you don't destroy the point (Fig. 2-6b); (5) carefully and slowly push this pointed end through the needle until about 1/16 in. (about 0.2 cm) is protruding from the other side of the eye; (6) very cautiously pull out this short end with your fingertips (or still better, with your fingernails), so the needle is safely on the thread; (7) if needed for

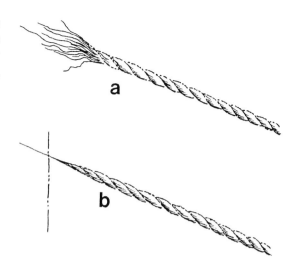

Fig. 2-6. *Preparing a thread end for threading a needle. (a) Break the thread rather than cut it. (b) After waxing the thread end, shape a pointed tip and cut off the fine end.*

a bead thread, pull half of it through the needle's eye and fold both halves around the eye (for a single thread just pull some 3 in. (7.5 cm); (8) again pull the full length of the doubled (or single) thread several times through the beeswax cake, taking care not to bend the fine needle; (9) pull the waxed thread several times between your fingertips to distribute the wax evenly and remove hard particles of wax.

Especially when doing lane-stitch beadwork, the thread may wear thin at the needle's eye, and if you encounter a stubborn spot of leather, the thinned thread is very likely to break. Repeated scooping of beads with tiny holes, and the many passages of the thread through the leather naturally strain a thread, no matter how well-waxed it was. If this happens, remove the beading needle, wax the end of the doubled thread and cut at an oblique angle; after smoothing the end between your fingertips, thread it through a sewing needle with a larger eye, repeat the stitch you wanted to make before the break (if you had beads on the thread), and fasten it with a few backstitches. Then start with a new thread, using the beading needle again and continue your work where you had to interrupt it.

SEWING THREAD ENDS. A knot alone does not secure the end of a new thread; no matter how much you pull, the end will have some

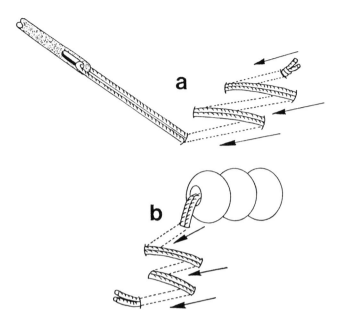

Fig. 2-7. Handling thread ends. (a) Sewing down thread end when starting a new thread. (b) Sewing down thread end when thread is used up.

leeway which will add up during the later work. Make the first stitch near the point where your beading starts, with the last of two or three backstitches emerging exactly at the designated spot. With this method no knot is needed at all, but a knot might help to stop the thread when you pull it through the leather for its first passage.

With each row beaded, the bead thread becomes shorter and shorter, until leaving about 6 in. (15 cm) between the last row and the needle; then it should be terminated with a few backstitches. At this end of the thread no knot is necessary at all, but you should take care to place these backstitches in an area where they will be concealed by future bead rows (Fig. 2-7).

3
TOOLS & PREPARATIONS

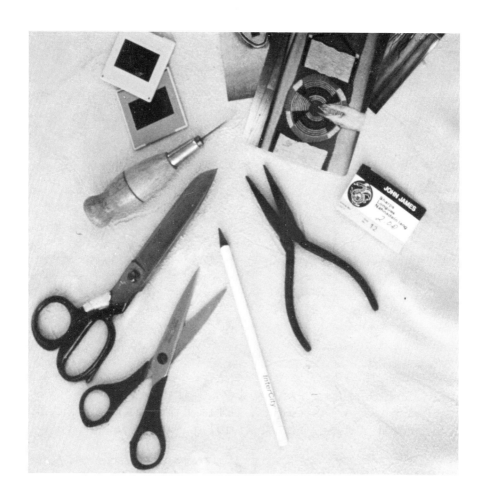

Today we have an array of tools at hand that the old-time beadworkers could only dream of, and I am sure they would have used all of them if they had been available. Of course, to be really authentic, we could turn back the wheel of time and use original tools only, as they were common in the 19th century. In fact, some trading posts offer such things for reenactments, but I doubt if they are used at the beadworker's home. And with public address systems in the dance arbor, with people using modern cars instead of horses to get to the powwows, I see nothing wrong in using modern tools to create traditional beadwork.

TOOLS

PENCILS VERSUS BALLPOINTS.   For many years I had strongly objected to ballpoint pens and used pencils to mark the lines necessary for lanes or primary designs. But one day I decided to give it a try, and *very lightly* drew the lines with a *black* ballpoint pen; while beading the piece I took care to conceal the lines within the stitches so they would be covered by the beads. Because I have seldom hurried my beadwork and have made it a habit to work simultaneously on different projects, most of them took several months to get finished. During that time the areas still unbeaded had been exposed to sunlight which faded the black lines to a pale reddish brown, resembling very closely the markings on an unfinished museum piece I know. Some of the lines even faded so much that I had to redraw them, which, however, is better than drawing a strong line from the start. Practicing on a piece of scrap will help you to get the right feel for it.

Pencils are fine for drawing lines if you prefer them; what I want to point out is that black ballpoint pens are not as bad as they may seem. The use of felt-tipped pens, though, should be discouraged; lines drawn with them are very likely to bleed when they get wet; and they will not fade.

SCISSORS. Three types of scissors should be used for working with beads: a small one for cutting threads and for fine repair work; a larger one for cutting cloth and leather; and a third one for cutting paper, such as paperbacking, patterns or stencils. Do not use the cloth or leather scissors for cutting paper—within a short time its blades will be dulled because of the pulp which is in the newsprint or paper bags.

NEEDLES. As a principle, use the smallest needle possible for any type of sewing or beading; the smaller the needle the easier it is to work with it. For sewn beadwork I always have favored the *sharps*, short fine needles with thin eyes. Normally, the size of a beading needle should correspond directly to the bead size it is used for. A #12 needle works fine with 12/o and 13/o beads. Once in a while, you might break or bend a needle, or the needle may lose its "bite" after constant use, so have a good supply at hand. For woven beadwork and the various types of gourd-stitch bead-

Fig. 3-1. *Needles used for the various techniques of Indian-style beadwork. (a) "Sharps" of size 12 are recommended for most of the sewn techniques with seed beads. (b) Long needles are useful for gourd-stitch beadwork and bead-weaving.*

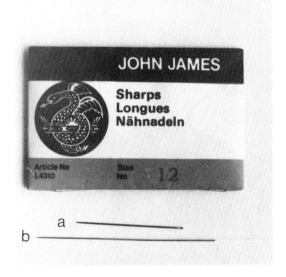

work you need long, thin needles which come in sizes between #13 and #16 (Fig. 3-1).

AWLS. If you have good buckskin to bead on, you will need an awl only the few times when you encounter a stubborn spot. Rawhide and stiff harness leather, of course, have to be pre-punched to get through with the needle, as I have detailed in the section on rawhide. Use a store-bought thin awl, or make your own by driving an appropriately-sized sewing needle eye-first into a piece of dowel or other wooden handle. Clamp the needle, eye up, in a vise so that about 1/4 in. (0.5 cm) projects upward and carefully tap the handle down onto it. By tapping this handle in several small increments, the needle can be forced well up into the wood, whereas trying to do it all at once will surely result in a broken needle.

A thin awl also is a very handy tool when you have to break poorly-shaped or surplus beads (you can also use a regular sewing needle which is bigger than your bead needle). In a bead row already sewn down, put the point of the awl in the bead hole, while your fingernail presses against the opposite side of the bead, and press the awl into the hole; on an open thread with beads strung, press the awl into the hole of offending bead while holding the thread taut (Fig. 3-2). The bead will split in two neat pieces, one of which is usually under the thread and can be easily

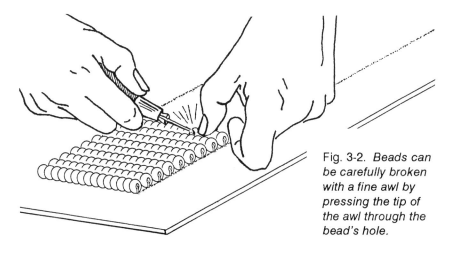

Fig. 3-2. *Beads can be carefully broken with a fine awl by pressing the tip of the awl through the bead's hole.*

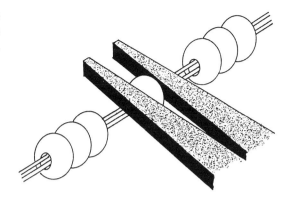

Fig. 3-3. *Flat-nosed pliers provide another method to break beads.*

flipped out with the tip of the awl. There is very much less chance of damaging the thread with this method than with the pliers method described below, and the broken piece won't fly in your eye.

NEEDLE-NOSED OR FLAT-NOSED PLIERS. Although using an awl, as described before, seems to be a more traditional way of breaking poorly-shaped or surplus beads, you may prefer pliers for this job. Isolate the bead to be removed between from its neighbors so a fair amount of thread on both sides of the bead is exposed; place the noses of the pliers around the bead and carefully squeeze them together (Fig. 3-3). To prevent cutting the thread keep the thread stretched taut with the bead resting on your index finger. Of course, you should protect your eyes by closing them or looking away while breaking the bead.

No matter how soft the buckskin used for your beadwork may be, once in a while you will encounter a stubborn spot, so your pliers will help to pull the beading needle through.

THIMBLES. Having been used to bead on buckskin as soft as flannel throughout the years, I have never felt the need to put a thimble on my finger; and I never have worried about callouses caused by constantly pushing the needle through the leather. Because the middle finger aids the thumb and index finger when pushing the needle through the leather or fabric, you simply have to feel the needle's eye on the bare tip of this finger to ensure the accurate length of each stitch.

There may be some relief, however, for beadworkers with tender finger tips: quilters sometimes use thimbles made of soft leather which come in three different sizes. Although more suited to quilting patchwork in an up-and-down fashion, the soft thimble may perhaps protect your finger tip.

Many beadworkers use a "rubber finger," a soft rubber sleeve that fits over the finger. Worn on the middle finger of the needle hand, it may help to give a better grip on the needle, especially in pulling it through the buckskin.

As with many novelty goods of Euro-American manufacture, brass thimbles were extremely popular among the Indian women who immediately found a different use for them: by drilling a hole at the top, these were hung as a series of bells to highlight fringes on women's skin and cloth dresses, or to string them on top of ribbon streamers which embellished bandoliers or cradle covers, to name only a few objects.

DOING BEADWORK ON FRAMES?   Frankly, I hate to see this issue in this book, but I've heard horror tales of people beading Sioux-style dress yokes on frames six feet long and almost three feet wide. Except perhaps for hoops to bead small rosettes, frames have only disadvantages and I see nothing good coming from them: you have to get lumber and construct the frame; no matter what the size, frames are extremely awkward to handle; you can't take them with you while traveling; to do lane-stitch beadwork, you have to stitch all the way through the leather and back, because you cannot hold the leather at the spot where you would pass the needle beneath the surface only, as it is correctly done with that technique; being stretched on the frame, the leather cannot give while being beaded—when you remove the finished piece from the frame, the bead rows most likely will pucker as the leather contracts to its previous size; last but not least the idea of beading on frames is ridiculous, it simply was not done and need not be done! Place your piece in your lap or on the tabletop and you will very quickly learn how to handle it.

When cutting out the buckskin piece which is to be beaded, you should leave an additional margin of an inch or so, which will be trimmed off when the beadwork is finished. That most articles are beaded before they are sewn together should go without saying—but I have seen a number of non-Indian-made objects completely sewn together but with the beadwork unfinished yet. As it is very difficult to handle a finished article and bead it at the same time, think about each step up to completion and where the beading fits into the process, before you start a project.

MEASUREMENTS AND DIMENSIONS

Before the late 1970's, beadworkers searching for patterns of 19th century Indian clothing and accoutrements often were left vague about the correct dimensions. This situation only improved when lavishly-illustrated exhibition and museum catalogs, and journals such as the *American Indian Art Magazine* became available to a wider public. Since the aesthetic composition depends to a great deal on the correct proportions of any given piece, proper measurements and dimensions should be considered in particular. Too often, non-Indian beadworkers seem to think that "bigger must be better." Proper sizes, however, are only half of the story—objects as well as designs followed prescribed aspect ratios which, over generations, have been shaped by an inborn artistic sense and tradition. An example which comes from the Crow should illustrate this point: diamonds usually have an aspect ratio of 1:3, with their long axis being three times as long as the short one; bases of tall, slender triangles amount to one half of their long axis, or to an aspect ratio of 1:2. Do not forget, however, that these are only clues and should not be taken as absolute; the aspect ratio of diamonds may also be 1:2.8 or 1:3.2, but they still are in the range of 1:3.

I will present two methods to determine dimensions which come very close to the original item: the first is using a slide projector, and the second uses rule-of-three calculations. In a few instances we can only approximate the original dimensions, because it is very difficult to tell if 12/o, 13/o, or 14/o beads, for example, were used. So if your results make no sense because they seem to be too large, recalculate on the basis of smaller beads (or vice versa). Remember that the bead size number defines the number of rows covering one inch (2.54 cm), so you would be well advised to include an inch or centimeter ruler whenever you take pictures in museums and/or private collections. But as most of your slides or prints very likely will have been photographed without such a ruler, you will need for either method a sample lane of roughly 3 in. (7.5 cm) length; preferably this lane should be beaded with 13/o beads, so you have some leeway for 12/o or 14/o beads, if recalculations should be necessary. A lane-stitched sample piece will also do for overlay or Crow-stitch work, as you need the bead *rows* only for reference.

MEASUREMENTS DETERMINED WITH SLIDE PROJECTOR. For this method you will need: (1) a clear and well-focused slide with the object filling the frame if possible; (2) a slide projector; (3) a chair with a flat seat; (4) drawing paper larger than you expect the object to be; (5) the sample piece; (6) a numbered color code of all bead colors found on the item. You should work in a room that can be darkened, or do this work at night.

Place the slide projector on the chair seat, put in the slide, and find a convenient surface to throw the image onto, such as a blank wall or a door (Fig. 3-4). Before doing the fine adjustments, turn on the projector to see where to mount the drawing paper with masking tapes. This accomplished, place your sample piece on the image, trying to align it with the projected bead rows. Move the chair and refocus until you feel really sure that the bead rows of the image and sample perfectly coincide. Before you continue, you should consult your literature for similar objects, to see if the found size makes sense. If there is too much discrepancy, adjust for a bigger or smaller bead size; i.e., "ignore" the sample lane now and use common sense.

Turn off the light, and with a well-sharpened pencil trace all important lines on the paper: outlines of the whole object, lanes, primary designs as well as smaller designs. If there are single row outlines, define them as such. In small design elements you even might mark individual bead rows with small dashes. Write the

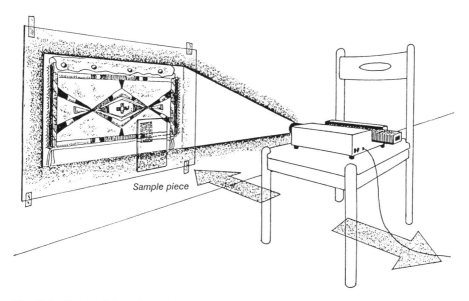

Fig. 3-4. *Determining dimensions with a slide projector.*

names of the colors, or the numbers of your color code into the appropriate fields.

Utmost care should be taken not to shove the chair out of its position while doing this work, because it is very difficult to readjust the image to lines already drawn. By blocking parts of the projection with your shadow, you can see if you have completed the drawing. When you have finished this work and turned on the light, you should have a decent drawing which you can use as a reference throughout your beading. Probably turning out less than perfect in terms of accuracy, the drawing will reveal the small imperfections inherent to native beadwork, contrasting some non-Indian beadwork which is done so meticulously that it almost looks machine-made (SMITH *B* 1983:65).

MEASUREMENTS BY CALCULATION.   Printed illustrations as they may be found in books, magazines, or catalogs, ask for a different approach and some calculation, so a pocket calculator might come in handy. This method may even work when absolutely no measurements are given, but I have to admit that it is more suited to

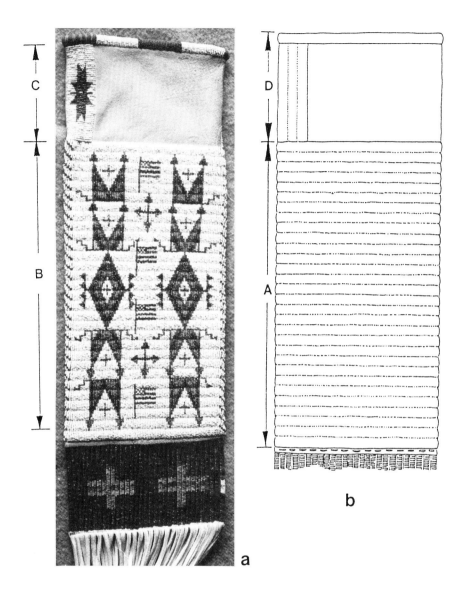

Fig. 3-5. *Determining the dimensions needed by calculations with the rule-of-three. (a) Illustration from which the measurements are taken: "B" represents the length of the beaded panel in the photograph; "C" stands for another length measured in the photograph. (b) Measurements on the object to be beaded: "A" represents the length figured out by counting beads and/or bead rows; "D" is the length which should correspond to "C".*

calculations with decimal fractions than with true fractions, commonly used to denote lengths in inches.

I would like to illustrate this method by using a reproduction to simulate a real Sioux pipe bag. In clear and detailed illustrations, the beads of an individual row can be counted easily. If this should not be possible because of the picture's poor quality, examine the design more closely. In Sioux-style beadwork, the diagonal design lines often are divided into three more-or-less tall steps within a lane, very often indicating three beads per step which would make nine beads per lane row; you have to look really carefully, and a magnifying glass or thread-counter might be useful. On your test piece, determine the length of a nine-beads row (do not forget the typical Sioux arch in lanes, making the lane a bit narrower). Multiplying the lane-width by the number of lanes gives you the first length needed for the further calculations.

Staying with the example (which, of course, is a bit idealistic—real situations will make calculations not always that easy), and assuming that the pattern bag was beaded with 13/o beads, we have counted nine beads per row which make a lane of about 1/2 in. (1.2 cm) width. Multiplied by 30 lanes makes an actual height of about 14 1/4 in. (36.2 cm) for the beaded panel, which will be our reference length *"A"*, from which all other measurements can be deduced. This beaded panel in the illustration (Fig. 3-5) is 3 in. (7.6 cm) high *("B")*, while the short upper part of the bag *"C"* measures one inch (2.54 cm) in the photograph. To find *"D"*, which represents the actual dimension corresponding to *"C"*, use the rule-of-three method or the following formula:

$$\frac{A \ \times \ C}{B} = \frac{36.2 \text{ cm} \ \times \ 2.54 \text{ cm}}{7.6 \text{ cm}} = D = 12.07 \text{ cm}$$

This procedure can be used for many different examples; if one dimension (usually height/length or width) is already given, you don't have to count beads and can use this measurement as reference for *"A"*, with its illustrated length being *"B"*. All other dimensions you are looking for will be *"D"* deduced from *"C"*.

If you have crooked or curvilinear lines, take a piece of thread, put a mark on it, and lay it carefully along the corresponding lines.

Its length can be taken from the straightened thread and will be your factor "*B*." You perhaps will need some imagination when doing such calculations or use a different approach to get measurements which come closest to the original item, but if you want to make faithful reproductions of old-time beadwork, this preliminary work is of utmost importance, and almost always the rule-of-three will be very useful for this job.

4
LANE-STITCH

Most people, if asked which Indian beading technique comes first to their mind, will answer invariably, "the lazy-stitch." In fact, this method of sewing beads onto a surface has been so common among craftspeople of many tribes on the Great Plains as well as the Plateau region that, of the various beading techniques, it has gained the widest recognition among admirers of Native American art. It is said to have its origins in two well-known quillwork embroidery techniques known as "parallel wrap technique" and "zigzag wrap technique." While not disputing the precedence of these quilling techniques and their impact on later Plains beaded art, I would like to point to beadworkers of the South African *Ndebele* who have covered large panels with series of lanes—beaded with bold, angular designs well-suited to the technique; in earlier times they even used sinew to string the beads on. Being an old tradition of their tribe, it can be doubted that the Ndebele ever had been exposed to Sioux or Cheyenne beadwork, or even influenced by it.

Instead of describing a beading technique precisely, the name "lazy-stitch" reflects White ethnocentrism, though most people who use this term probably are not aware of this connotation. No matter how easy and fast this beading technique may have been, it took perseverance and many back-breaking hours to produce such prestigious objects as fully-beaded cradle covers, or the yokes of women's ceremonial dresses. You hardly would call a woman *lazy* who devotes almost two years to making a fully-beaded suit of vest and trousers for her adoptive son (HABERLAND D 1986:89). To embroider an object with more than 200,000 beads is a challenge with any technique, not to be denigrated by derogatory terms as "lazy-stitch" or even "lazy-squaw-stitch."

For that very reason I will use, throughout this book, the neutral and more descriptive term *lane-stitch*; only when I have to quote from sources will I reluctantly resort to the old name. Bill Holm, who is to be credited for introducing "lane-stitch," writes:

> I have little illusion that such hard-core terms as lazy-stitch can be replaced, but it shouldn't be impossible. For over three hundred years the arctic natives of North America have been known as *Eskimo*. Within the last ten years, in Canada, that name has been entirely replaced by *Inuit*. Admittedly the native population, the government, educators and the media all cooperated, but millions of Canadians changed a centuries-old habit. A fifty year-old term known to a few thousand people ought not to be that firmly ensconced! (HOLM F 1984:28)

KNOW YOUR BEADS!

When you bead with Italian beads (or modern reproductions of the old colors) you will notice that, even within the same size, beads of some colors may be rather narrow, while the beads' length of another color may be a little bit larger. One batch of 13/o beads may appear as 12/o, while the next 13/o color might come closer to 14/o; you always will have to allow some tolerances in beads. "Old-style" beadwork done with perfectly shaped and uniform beads looks so artificial and nondescript that you can almost forget about it. Modern style beadwork, on the other hand, with its bold designs and daring color combinations, might profit from these very beads, so just collect your colors and don't worry about "old-time" beadworkers' concerns!

As long as backgrounds, block designs, or smaller design elements are created by solidly-colored lane-wide rows, slightly different beads will not affect the work. ("Row" should be defined as a given number of beads on the same thread between two opposite stitches.) But you may run into problems when beading, say, a royal blue triangle in a field of pink beads, if these beads have different dimensions; while the center row of the triangle may have the exact number of beads planned for the lane width, two or even three more beads could be needed to fill the length of a bead row in the background, depending on the bead shapes. As

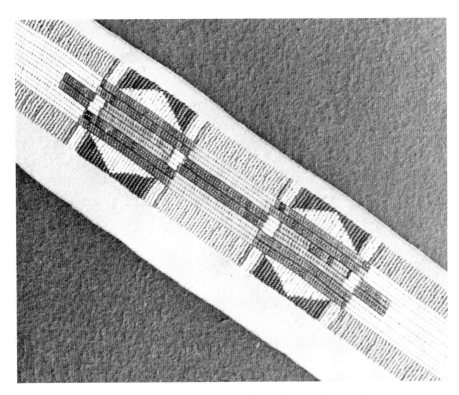

Fig. 4-1. *When beads began to appear on the Plains and the Plateau, they were only sparingly used to augment the quillwork that prevailed in the early 19th century. Here a quill-wrapped horsehair shirt-strip in the Umatilla style is bordered by seed-bead lanes (Quillwork and beadwork by the author).*

a consequence, beading smooth diagonal lines for the triangles may turn out to be difficult.

If you are not yet familiar with your beads, I would suggest that you make a short sample lane, beading a row for each color you have selected for your lane-stitch project (or even for all colors you have collected). Also add a simple design with a diagonal line in it, to see if you will have to compensate for different widths of beads. Inspect each color carefully and note if you have to add or omit beads to fit the row into the lane width. Whenever you buy new beads, you should examine their size and shape, and compare them with the beads you already have.

DRAWING GUIDELINES

Several important factors affect the widths of lanes: the style of beadwork chosen; the objects the lanes are beaded on; and the size of the beads used for lane-stitch work. On most Sioux-style beadwork you will find lanes eight or nine, sometimes even ten to twelve, beads wide. If you are using stepped designs, it is much easier if the steps come out even with the lane edges; i.e., an even number of beads works best with an even number of steps (2 or 4) while 3 steps in a lane work better with 6, 9, or 12 beads in a row.

Beadwork of the Crow and Plateau Indians uses lanes primarily for bordering flat panels, and here the individual rows of a lane sometimes may contain 15 to 20 beads, depending on the objects; Southern Plains beadwork, on the other hand, often favors narrow, isolated lanes which may be just five to six beads wide.

Once you have decided on the design and the width of the lanes, draw all "lane-lines," using a ruler to assure straight lines. Draw these lines only very lightly with your ballpoint or pen pencil, so you have a reference where to place your stitches.

As lane-stitch beading largely is a matter of counting rows and beads, there is no need to draw guidelines for the designs themselves. Actually, you should not do this, because your *beaded* designs most likely will not coincide with all lines of your *drawn* designs. I will return to this subject in detail when designs are discussed; for explaining the basic technique of the lane-stitch, guidelines for the lanes are the only ones needed.

HOW TO HOLD YOUR WORK

Although the first lane can be started either at the top or bottom of the piece, for three reasons you should start with the lowermost lane: this lane will be the nearest to your body, with the remainder of the skin lying on the tabletop or in your lap; to facilitate holding the piece in your hand while you insert the needle, you can fold over the leather near the lane you are beading; for the subsequent

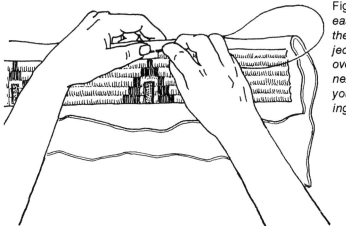

lanes it is easier to insert the needle along the upper edge of the previous lane than below its lower edge (Fig. 4-2).

On a really large piece, however, such as a fully-beaded Sioux-style dress yoke, it might be better to start with the lanes running along the shoulders and the neck opening, thus forming sort of "center lanes." As both areas are to be filled with lanes, these "center lanes" function as bottom lanes for both panels. Remember to have always an edge, or more likely a fold, near the lane you are beading. Working with the lane-stitch technique this way is much easier than fighting with awkward frames.

BASIC TECHNIQUE

To start the first bead row in a lane, mark the points for the beginning of the thread and the opposite stitch clearly to make the row lying perfectly at a right angle to the pre-drawn lane-lines. Fasten the thread end between the lane-lines with a few back-stitches so it emerges at the lower of the two markings. After the number of beads needed for a complete row has been picked up, place the first stitch at the opposite mark, taking a stitch-length of a bead's diameter or just a tiny bit longer (Fig. 4-3a). At the same time, taking care that the needle travels along the outer border of the lane-line helps to conceal this lane-line under the beads (Fig.

4-4c). While pulling the thread entirely through and tugging it taut, hold down the bead row with your index finger and press it against the leather; doing so with each bead row aligns them neatly.

Instead of stitching all the way through the buckskin and back, the needle just catches its upper surface and the thread or sinew runs under the surface of the leather (Fig. 4-3c); no exposed stitches can be seen on the backside of the leather. As there is no rule without an exception, you may sometimes find authentic lane-stitch work with the stitches going all the way through the leather (Fig. 4-3d). Due to the constant pulling of the bead thread, the buckskin will be contracted a little bit along the stitches and will show dips or furrows. When beading on cloth, canvas, rawhide, or stiff commercial leather, however, the thread must go

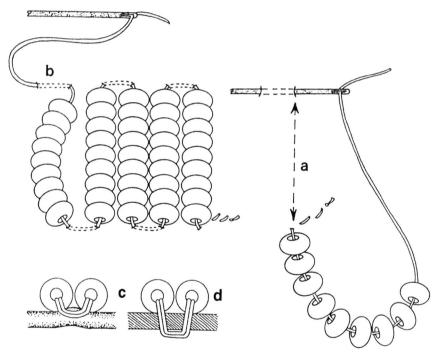

Fig. 4-3. *Basic technique of the lane-stitch. (a) Place the first stitch exactly opposite the spot the thread emerges from. (b) Anchoring of a bead row. (c) When beading on buckskin, just catch the surface of the leather with the needle. (d) On cloth, rawhide, and harness leather, the thread has to go completely through the material and back.*

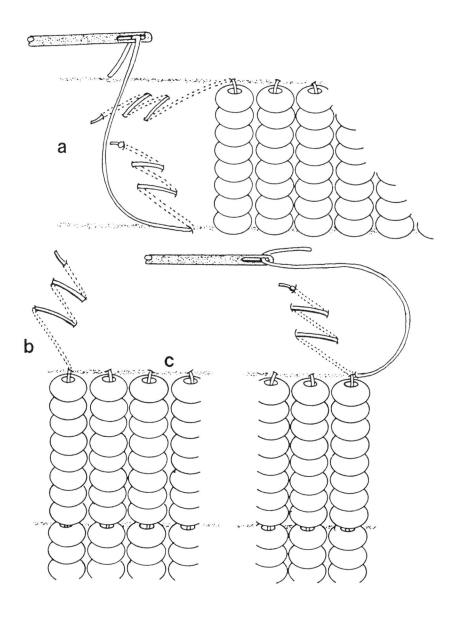

Fig. 4-4. *Sewing thread end in lane-stitch beadwork. (a) Within a lane when a new thread is needed. (b) Finishing a lane and starting a new lane. (c) Placing the stitches on the outside of the guideline.*

completely through the material and return through it and you even have to prepunch holes in the case of the latter two.

To sew down the second bead row, insert the needle on the opposite marking line—the line on which you started your first row—approximately a half bead-width away from the previous row, and emerge with the needle in a distance of one bead's width. It might even be suggested, when working on buckskin, to make this stitch slightly longer than one bead's width, otherwise the rows will be too crowded—a mistake commonly found among beginning lane-stitchers. From now on, lane-stitch beading largely is a matter of sewing down bead rows in a "zigzag" fashion (Fig. 4-3b), placing the stitches alternatingly on both lane-lines. (Don't take "zigzag" too literally, though!)

When your thread becomes too short to be used conveniently, sew the end down *between* the marking lines; start the new thread near the old one, and, with the last backstitch, come out exactly at the point where you would continue your work (Fig. 4-4a). How to sew down threads at the end of a lane depends on the type of your beadwork. (1) On a multiple lane panel, sew the ends of the old and the new threads between the lines of the next lane: this way the backstitches will be covered by the bead rows of the next lane (Fig. 4-4b). (2) If you bead a single lane only, you either can sew the thread end on the backside of the leather, or you can place the backstitches so that they will be covered by the last rows of the lane.

ARCHED AND FLAT LANES

In a typical lane, the individual bead rows tend to arch or bulge upward slightly rather than lie completely flat. Sioux beadwork, however, very often featured extremely arched lanes; this effect was achieved by placing the opposite stitches closer together than the number of beads in the row would normally allow; i.e., nine beads for example were used for a row instead of the eight beads that would fit into the space available. If you plan to reproduce classic Sioux-style beadwork, you should take this feature into account when you draw the lane-lines. Even though the lane-stitch was called "hump-stitch" by the Sioux (POWERS C 1986: 138), they surely did not do all of their beadwork with such extremely arched lanes; much of it displays gently arched lanes only (Fig. 4-5a).

The Cheyenne, on the other hand, have been known for beading lanes which lie completely flat on the buckskin; perfect alignment of the bead rows with those of the adjacent lanes is another hallmark of classic Cheyenne beadwork. This flat effect was achieved by passing the thread *behind* two bead rows of the previous lane, and, at the same time, through the leather. In other words, the bead thread was "hooked" into the neighboring bead rows (Fig. 4-5b). Tugging the rows taut puts additional tension on the rows in the adjacent lane, thus adding to their flat appearance.

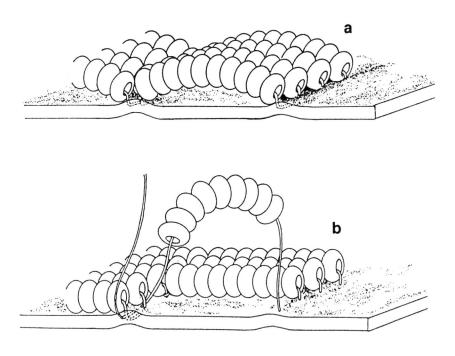

Fig. 4-5. *In lane-stitch beadwork, the bead rows could be either arched or completely flat. (a) Arched rows of typical Sioux-style beadwork, with the stitch placed next to the previous lane. (b) Flat lanes as found often in Cheyenne-style beadwork, with the thread "hooked" into the previous lane.*

A few beadworkers of the Southern Cheyenne in Oklahoma, making moccasins and other objects for trade, have been reported to pass the thread behind the bead rows of the neighboring lane only, *without* going through the leather at all. Far from criticizing an Indian practice, I would not recommend this method, as the friction caused by the two threads rubbing together puts too much strain on the threads and eventually may break them (STEWART *D* 1971 b:6).

However, much of the old Cheyenne beadwork does not make use of this particular "hooking" technique. As with the arched lanes of Sioux beadwork, it shows the possible variations of a technique within a tribe and you should not draw the conclusion that these variations were used exclusively by the respective tribes only because they have been associated with them.

ORGANIZATION OF LANES

LANE PANELS. The Sioux, Cheyenne, as well as the Arapaho used the lane-stitch almost exclusively to fill entire panels with lanes. Most often, these lanes crossed the main axis of the primary design(s) beaded into them. Because the individual bead rows thus parallelled the main axis of the design, the furrows clearly visible between the lanes counterbalanced the design optically. On moccasins, the placement of the border lanes was dictated by the shape of the object; but even here most designs *crossed* the lanes with their axis. As I have seen on a number of reproductions, this interplay between lanes and designs is very easily overlooked by many a non-Indian beadworker trying to emulate this beadwork style (Figs. 4-8 and 4-9).

Whether the lanes run horizontally or vertically, depends on how the object is positioned: on spread-out war shirts, as they are often displayed in museums, the lanes on the sleeve strips appear horizontal; however, if you imagine how such a shirt is worn on the body with the arms hanging down, these lanes run vertically.

In Crow-style beadwork, the lanes had a completely different function: they bordered solidly beaded areas done in overlay or

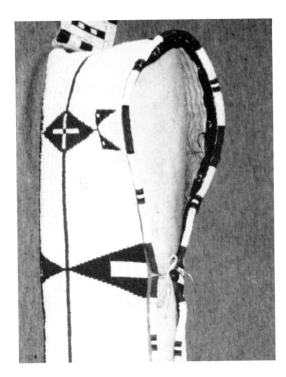

Fig. 4-6. *Sioux cradle cover, with the lanes crossing the main axis of the primary designs (Holm collection; photograph by Bill Holm).*

Crow-stitch, and on large panels such as cradle tops or horse collars they very often divided them (Fig. 4-8).

ISOLATED LANES. Very often parallel lanes were beaded isolated from each other, with a certain amount of the foundation material visible between them. Sacred beadwork of the Cheyenne and Arapaho is a typical example for this style of lane-stitch beading and was used on tipi equipment such as covers, door flaps, linings, and pillows.

Among the Crow, separately beaded lanes were commonly used on tipi bags (Fig. 4-9). Women's "wedding robes" were almost exclusively decorated this way, with some of them featuring diamonds beaded so cleverly as if they were seen through a half-open venetian blind (MERRITT *F* 1988).

While some lane-stitch work covering full panels was done by the Southern Plains tribes, their beadwork is characterized by

single, narrow lanes with intricate designs. These lanes usually bordered large areas of skin painted green or yellow.

TAPERING LANES. The Crow and the Plateau beadworkers used to highlight their primary designs with tapering lanes of dark blue or red beads, thus creating "border frames" (Fig. 4-10). Further examples of tapering lanes include small triangles or diamonds (often called "feather motifs") with their apexes abutting the fully-beaded main area (Fig. 4-10). These small elements usually start with one or two beads at the apex, with each succeeding row increasing by one bead; with some experience you will be able to bead such small designs without drawing any guidelines.

CURVED LANES. Lane-stitch beadwork usually consists of straight lanes maintaining their width throughout their length. Many objects, however, call for lanes changing their course, and, in some cases, even their width: in "representational beadwork," which

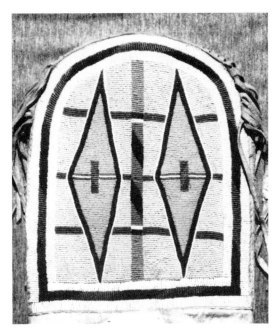

Fig. 4-8. *Beaded top of a Crow cradle-board, surrounded by three lanes and divided by a vertical lane into two panels—a typical usage of lanes in Crow-style beadwork (Honnen collection; photograph by Bill Holm).*

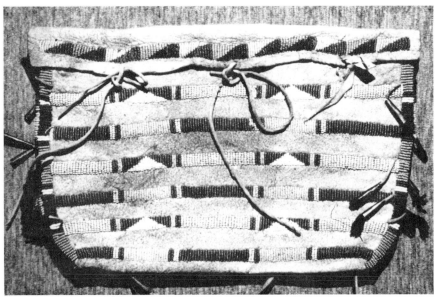

Fig. 4-9. *Tipi bags were one of the few objects where the Crow beadworkers beaded lanes exclusively (Honnen collection; photograph by Bill Holm).*

Fig. 4-10. *Tapering lanes are often found on Transmontane-style beadwork as on this reproduction of a Crow lance-case flap. Note how the lanes in the border frames or the appending triangles vary their widths (Beadwork by the author).*

became popular in the Reservation period, the lanes often followed the contours of motifs such as warriors with feather bonnets, or men on horseback (Fig. 4-13). You will find this type of beadwork on fully-beaded men's vests, "scout" jackets, or on pipe bags.

On Blackfeet and Plateau women's hide and cloth dresses, the yokes were decorated with a series of wide lanes which curved in the center on both the chest and back (resembling an expanded "W" in some way), and tapered towards the yoke's ends (Fig. 4-11). While pony beads were used as a rule for these dresses, the Blackfeet quite often replaced them by "basket" or "bugle" beads. Even wide lanes of small seed beads were not uncommon, and no measures were taken to secure them additionally between the rows' ends.

SHARP CURVES IN LANES. Sometimes, as on the toes of moccasins, the lanes must run in sharp curves. To bead them as uniformly as possible, you have to make smaller stitches on the inside curve and wider stitches on the outside curve, with their lengths depending on the sharpness of the curve. Know well ahead

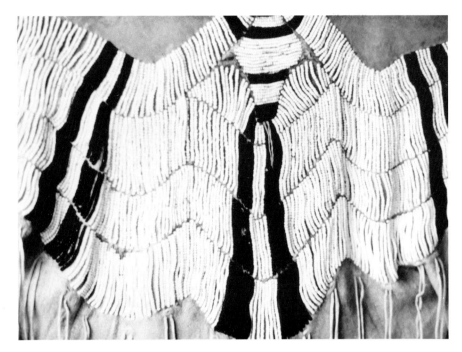

Fig. 4-11. *Wide, curved lanes were an outstanding feature of the hide dresses worn by the women of the Plateau tribes (Honnen collection).*

when to start beading a sharp curve so you can make the transition as smooth as possible. In very sharp curves such as the innermost lane of a moccasin toe, it may be necessary to shorten a few of the bead rows by one or even more beads (Fig. 4-12).

LANE-STITCH DESIGNS

In the early period of lane-stitch beading, designs usually consisted of simple block designs which were accomplished by bead rows of different colors. In later times, more complex figures and ornaments were created by changing the colors *within* a bead row, depending on the chosen designs; in other words, design and background were beaded at the same time. The angle of the sides of triangles or diamonds—or any oblique design element—was

Fig. 4-12. *When beading sharp curves, stitches on the outer perimeter of the lane must be longer than those on its inner perimeter.*

limited by the number and size of beads forming the steps of diagonal lines and borders.

Time and again, you will find, even in recent publications, lane-stitch beadwork associated with geometric designs only. Too many examples, however, of representational beadwork from the tribes who have been known for their strictly geometric style, show images of mounted warriors and horses with separately beaded lanes running in different directions and varying their widths, depending on the parts of the image (Figs. 4-13 & 4-14).

Theoretically, most complicated flower designs could be executed with the lane-stitch in the way they would be done in petit-point embroidery. Some of the representational Sioux beadwork was actually done by changing the colors within the bead rows, thus integrating, for example, flowers and tendrils with the backgrounds. However, beading this type of beadwork by integrating designs and background does not seem to have been very common in the classic period, probably for aesthetic reasons. Straight lanes, with their furrows between them, seem much better suited for geometric designs, while the rows of overlay-stitch

Fig. 4-13. *Sioux pipe bag with representational beadwork: the lanes follow the contours of the animal and the warrior (Burke Museum, Seattle; photograph by Bill Holm).*

Fig. 4-14. *Beading the primary designs with lanes following their contours, as on this tipi bag, is a typical trait of Yanktonai beadwork (Ian M. West collection).*

beadwork, seen from a distance, blend into one surface, with its texture of straight bead rows harmonizing with the curved rows of the floral designs.

PLANNING YOUR DESIGNS

With beadwork designs around them anywhere and any time, the old-time craftswomen of the Sioux, Cheyenne, or Arapaho were so familiar with them that they could probably begin any piece of beadwork "off the cuff," having absorbed the components of the style over the generations. Most of us, however, have grown up in a totally different culture and environment, and each beadwork project is a new challenge—we have to grapple with the elements of a tribal style and its elements: designs, colors, placement, and arrangement.

For those reasons, it seems perfectly acceptable to plan the chosen designs carefully and to draw them with colored pencils on a "graph paper" (see appendix, page 194). Doing so, you get a very distinct idea of the characteristics of a typical Cheyenne or Sioux artifact, and, secondly, you can check your beadwork constantly against your drawing. By no means should you follow such a graph paper slavishly: any design or color change coming to your mind can be tested on paper before doing it with the beads. On the other hand, you should stick with the designs and colors painstakingly once you have decided upon them—most often your beadwork will not profit from last minute changes.

PANEL BELTS

As a rule, the basic technique of the lane-stitch and its variations were not influenced by the objects decorated with that technique, but the panel belts worn by the tribes of the Northern Plains and the Plateau use three more interesting variations of the lane-stitch.

These belts, which became popular during the late Reservation period, were almost always made from hard commercial leather, and were most often divided into seven sections or panels (hence the name "panel belt"). Three of these panels were decorated with beads: one in the back and two on the hips. As the leather bends when the belts are placed around the waist, the individual lane rows of the panels had to be longer than normally necessary so they could adapt and stretch over this curved surface; on a belt stretched out straight, these bead rows tend to sag (Fig. 4-16). The three beaded panels were further divided into three or five fields, often separated by vertical lines done in the overlay-technique. As the leather was too stiff for the delicate bead needles, an awl was needed to punch holes on a line pre-drawn with a pencil. Punching pairs of holes opposing each other helps to achieve a uniform distance between the holes.

Usually the bead rows in the border lanes of the panel belts were beaded at a right angle, using the regular lane-stitch, exposing the stitches on the belt's backside (Fig. 4-17a). On some belts, however, the holes on the edge were pierced at an angle of 45° so that the stitches ran along the narrow edge of the leather (Fig. 4-17b). Many of the tribes who made panel belts, such as the Crow or Flathead, had a predilection for beading slanted instead of

Fig. 4-15. *Various panel belts with some of them studded with brass tacks as was commonly done on this type of belts (Honnen collection).*

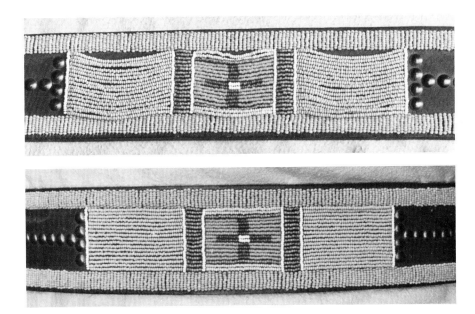

Fig. 4-16. *Panel belts. Top: The wide lanes of the panels were beaded quite loosely. Bottom: When worn around the waist, the loose bead rows tighten and form a smooth surface (Beadwork by the author).*

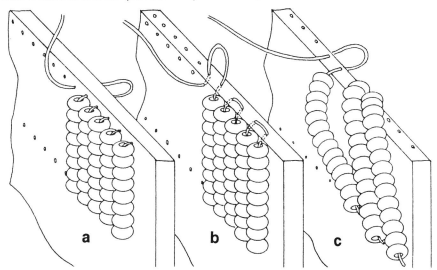

Fig. 4-17. *Different methods were used to bead the border lanes on panel belts. (a) Standard method. (b) Stitching through the edge of the leather. (c) Covering the belt's edge with the beads.*

vertical rows. In order to conceal the edges of the belt, which was a common feature of many panel belts with slanted bead rows in the border lanes, the holes were punched at an angle of about 45° from the edge through to the back side (Fig. 4-17c).

5
OVERLAY-STITCH

Across the whole North American continent—from the Micmac on the Eastern Seaboard to the Tlingit of Southeast Alaska, from the Seminole in the cypress swamps of Florida to the Athapaskan on the taigas of the subarctic North—a beading technique was widely distributed which is known by various names: *applique-stitch*, *spot-stitch*, *couching-stitch*, or *overlay-stitch*. It is the last of these terms that has stuck with most of us because it aptly describes its effect of coating an area with beads.

Being the most varied and versatile method for sewing beads on a leather or fabric surface, the overlay-stitch has been used for strictly geometric as well as for floral and figured designs. Santee beadworkers, for example, would embroider their filigreed flower designs on cloth or hide to make them stand out against the unbeaded background; for decorating her dress yokes or horse trappings, an Assiniboine woman would cover large panels solidly with beads, with the bead rows running at her will—vertically or horizontally, whichever fit better into the chosen design. Her choice might even be diagonal bead rows across the shoulder and sleeve strips of a man's shirt.

Contrary to popular belief, overlay beadwork, authentically done with *two* threads and needles, is no more difficult than the lane-stitch or Crow-stitch. It simply takes much more time to cover an entire area. If the *single-thread* method, sometimes called the "White Man's overlay-stitch," is not described in this chapter, it is because I will not include a beading technique that was *not* used by the Indians, its undeserved popularity among many non-Indian beadworkers notwithstanding!

Fig. 5-1. *Blackfeet woman's legging beaded with stepped triangles which are outlined with "checkerboard"-designs, a typical trait of the classic Blackfeet beading style (Museum für Völkerkunde, Freiburg, Germany).*

PAPERBACKING

Most often overlay work is done directly on buckskin or canvas. Sometimes, however, you may have to prevent your beading foundation from stretching or contraction. A practice already common among the Crow or Blackfeet craftswomen around the turn of the century and used even more so today is to sew on some *paperbacking* (LOEB F 1984a:135). On beadwork of the Canadian Cree Indians, the couching- or tacking-stitches are so tight that it is difficult to see any paper (DUNCAN H 1989:197).

Newspaper, or still better, the brown Kraft paper bags you have saved from your shopping errands, are ideal materials for paperbacking. For basting on the paper with a few running-stitches you have two options.

One has the paper lying on the upper surface of the leather, so you can draw your guidelines directly on the paper; when your

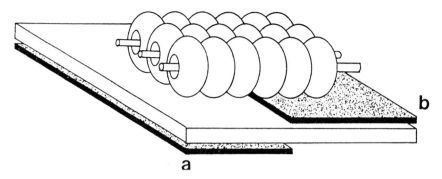

Fig. 5-2. *Paperbacking. (a) On the backside of the leather. (b) Between the beads and the leather.*

work is finished, the paper will be "sandwiched" between the beads and the leather (Fig. 5-2b). Much of the modern Crow overlay work is done that way. More frequently, though, the paper was fastened on the backside of the leather, as demonstrated by some pairs of Crow moccasins I have studied in museum collections (Fig. 5-2a). Several layers of newsprint support the beadwork on these moccasin vamps.

The stiff paper perhaps will not lend itself to a smooth beading when you do your first stitches. But with your repeated stitching through both the leather and paper, the paper soon will be quite perforated and the many creases caused by the constant handling of the beaded article will restore some of the paper's flexibility. When your beadwork is finished, simply tear away the excess paper as you would do with a postage stamp.

DRAWING GUIDELINES

In Northern Plains beadwork, geometric designs as a rule were embroidered with a fully-beaded background, and the most important markings to be pre-drawn are the border lines of the entire design field. There is no need, however, to cross every "t" and dot every "i" when you draw the design lines; the full-sized sketch you traced from a projected slide (see pages 46–47) should be your main reference to take measurements from. If lines or design perimeters coincide with the bead rows, you can make do with few markings, since the bead rows themselves provide some reference. You may draw lines which cross the bead rows at right and/or oblique angles to assure smooth delineations of pattern elements. I have used this method successfully when beading background and designs simultaneously. Restricting myself to the most necessary markings only, I more than once was able to make last minute corrections without spoiling the buckskin. Imagine that you have drawn two primary designs connected to each other, but suddenly decide to use your beadwork for something else which needs one primary design only: even lightly drawn pencil lines are sometimes hard to erase from the buckskin or cloth.

For flower designs, you may have to draw the lines for stalks and tendrils, as well as the outlines of petal and leaf elements. As in the example before, I would advise you to proceed slowly and bead one element only at a time, particularly if you should decide to leave the background unbeaded. Even when doing a close reproduction, you might come up with a different idea that blends well with the already finished part of your beadwork.

BASIC TECHNIQUE

No matter if you do geometric or floral designs, the first row you will bead is most important, because the quality of your finished beadwork depends on how carefully you sew down the beads in this very first line. It doesn't matter if you are right- or left-handed: one row will run from left to right, the next from right to left, and so forth. Normally you would expect to turn your work around after each row to maintain your working direction. Getting used, however, to keeping the work constantly in the same relation to your body will result in better crafts(wo)manship.

At one end of the perimeter line where you start your overlay work, fasten a *doubled* thread with a few backstitches; after the last backstitch it should emerge at the very end where the first row begins. Just to have a convenient name for this doubled thread, I will call this the *bead-thread* as the beads to be sewn down will be strung on it. Next to it, fasten the *tacking-thread* in the same

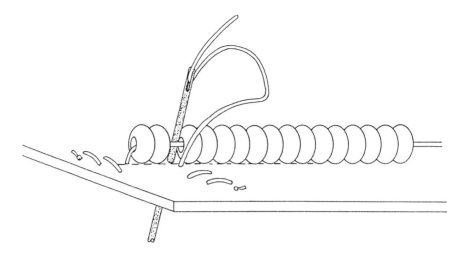

Fig. 5-3. *To start the overlay-stitch beading sequence, the needle is inserted on the other side of the bead-thread.*

fashion with backstitches (Fig. 5-3). Take care that it emerges two beads away from the first thread. Unlike the bead-thread, the tacking-thread is a *single* thread only. You might think that a doubled tacking-thread will lend more firmness to your beadwork; *it will not!* On the contrary, using a doubled tacking-thread is most likely to warp your finished piece beyond repair.

Unless your design starts on the very first row, string all beads of your chosen background color, depending on the length of the pre-drawn line; otherwise string only the beads of the first color needed plus a dozen more. (You will learn more about how to change colors later.) At the same time watch out for beads too oddly-shaped to be tolerated; if some should happen to be amidst the others, break them with your pliers, needle, or awl.

Instead of securing this row's end as you would do with a lane-stitch row, simply place the bead row on the line, with the needle lying on the table top or dangling over its edge. If you sewed it down, each of the tacking-stitches needed for one row would make the beads cramp more and more, until there would be no more room for them on the thread and you would have to break a number beads to slacken the thread. Leaving the needle

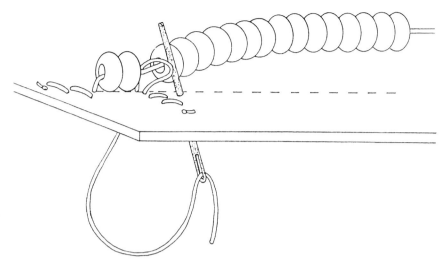

Fig. 5-4. *After pulling through most of the tacking-thread and just leaving a small loop, the needle is inserted from below, not more than two beads away.*

end free while sewing down the rows saves beads and makes your work easier.

If this is your first piece of overlay beadwork, proceed very, very slowly; think about each step and why you should do it that way—until it comes automatically and you have to force yourself to stop working. Soon you may be "hooked" to the rhythm of this technique and share some of the daily chores of an old-time Indian beadworker (Loeb *F* 1983:8).

With the bead row resting on the guideline, the tacking-thread should emerge from the leather on one side of the row, and, preferably, between the second and third bead. Just on the other side of the bead-thread and leaving no leeway for it, insert your needle and push it all the way through the leather. Carefully pull through most of the tacking-thread, leaving open a small half-inch (1 cm) loop which will be needed as a reference for the *return-stitch*.

If you never have done embroidery work on a hoop, doing this return-stitch as exactly as possible may be the most difficult operation of overlay beading, because you cannot see where to insert the needle from below (Fig. 5-4). But again, this is just a

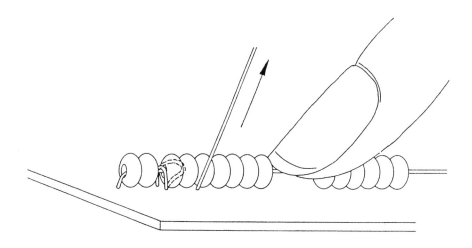

Fig. 5-5. *Pulling through all of the tacking-thread and thus closing the loop while pressing the beads against the loops completes the sequence.*

matter of experience and practice. After some two or three hundred return-stitches you will have forgotten thinking about and do it as if you had inherited that talent!

The small loop you left open will help you to find the exact spot; push the bead row a little bit aside to expose the pre-drawn guideline. From below, try to poke the needle through the leather, a distance of two beads away from the loop. If you miss it, do not despair, but try again—your fine needle won't damage the leather. Now that you have managed after many tries to find the right spot, pull the needle all the way through, together with a couple of inches of thread. With your fingernail press a half inch's (about 1 cm) length of beads against the loop and pull the rest of the tacking-thread, until the loop completely closes around the bead-thread and between the designated beads (Fig. 5-5). Each stitch you make will naturally put some pull on the previous stitches, so *there is absolutely no need to tug the tacking-thread* additionally! Actually, were you to do so, the tacking-thread would be drawn too close to the leather surface, thus causing dips in the bead row(s). The result would be an irregular surface, opposing the perfectly smooth effect you should strive for. As I said before, it may take a few hundred stitches to get the hang of it.

Your tacking-thread very likely will get twisted while sewing down the bead row. To untwist it, simply let the needle dangle and run the thread several times between your fingertips from its present end toward the needle. You may have to do this several times during a working session. Also, applying another wax coating helps to stabilize the tacking-thread.

For two reasons you should *not* be tempted to simply run the tacking-thread beneath the surface of your buckskin: first, it was not done; second, if you did, the pulling force of your tacking-thread would compress the leather along the bead row. Stitching twice through the leather puts some friction on the thread and acts as a "brake." I vividly remember beading my first pair of Crow-style moccasins many years ago. Not knowing better, I simply ran the tacking-thread beneath the leather's surface as I normally did with the lane-stitch. I surely learned the hard way when I came to realize that the vamp had shrunk across its width by almost half an inch (1 cm)!

The rest of the bead row is sewn down after every *second* bead. Except for the white single-row outlines common in Crow-style beadwork, by all means do resist the temptation to skip more than two beads when sewing down the first row! If you want first class quality, you should take the time and patience to bead the first row as smooth and straight as possible. In her outstanding analysis of Athapaskan beadwork, Kate Duncan says, "Contemporary beadworkers point to tight stitches, placed between each two beads, as characteristic of quality work" (DUNCAN H 1989:197). Designs can be off-balance to a certain degree which may add to your beadwork's authentic look, but your craftsmanship should be the best possible!

With the entire row sewn down and surplus beads removed, you have two options to fasten the bead-thread before starting the next row: (1) by using two additional tacking-stitches with the tacking-thread (Fig. 5-6a); (2) sewing it down as you would do with a single row in lane-stitch work (Fig. 5-6b). On most occasions the decision will be up to you, but when beading petals or leaves in floral beadwork, you may have to find out which of the two

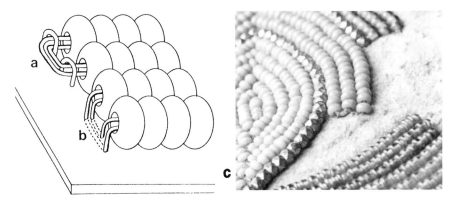

Fig. 5-6. *Two methods to finish a row can be used. (a) Two tacking-stitches sew down the bead-thread before it is turned for the next row. (b) Sewing down the row as in lane-stitch. (c) These floral designs use the first method of tacking down the end of a bead row.*

methods is better suited, depending if two rows simply align with each other as they do in geometric work or if they meet an angle as they would often do in floral beadwork (Fig. 5-6c).

BEADING THE NEXT ROWS

Thus far, you have learned almost all the fundamentals of the overlay-stitch. But I would like to share a few secrets with you which will help you to make overlay beadwork as good as the finest you have seen.

From now on, each new row is separated from the previous one by a groove; the new row's side next to the groove I will call the *groove-side*. Its other side, facing the wide open space of your leather or cloth backing, will be called the *open-side*. String your second row of beads and place it alongside the first one. Insert your needle from above on the *open-side* (Fig. 5-7a) and pull it through all the way except for the small loop which you should leave open. *Return* the needle from below on the *groove-side* (Fig. 5-7b), and while pressing a few beads against the loop, carefully pull up (Don't tug!) the rest of the tacking-thread. Now you are ready for the next stitches and rows.

When beading a stepped triangle in Blackfeet checkerboard fashion, for example, you might want to string all beads of the row in the color sequence required by the design. The first few stitches in the design area, however, will quickly shift the design sections out of their designated positions because of the space needed by the tacking-thread. A simple calculation will graphically show the tacking-stitches' impact on the position of the individual beads: the cotton thread I use has a width of roughly 1/64 in. (0.04 cm). If your design unit is, say, 26 beads long, you will have to tack it twelve times which, as a consequence, adds 1/8 to 3/16 in. (0.5 cm) to the design's intended length: in other words, your design unit would be at least three to four beads longer!

There is a better and easier way for changing colors within a row although it will entail repeated scooping. Just string a sufficient quantity of beads roughly equalling the length of your design unit and add a half inch (1 cm) of the same color. (These extra beads will be needed for pressing against the loops.) Tack down this section until its designated end. If the very last bead of this color should be too wide to align neatly with a crossing line, simply break it and take the next bead which may be narrower. Remove the excess beads you needed for pressing against the last loop, and string the next color to continue sewing down the bead row.

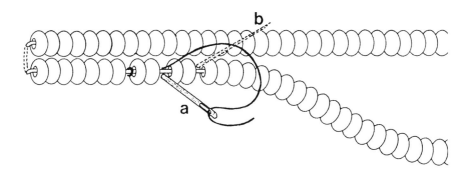

Fig. 5-7. *Sewing down subsequent bead rows in overlay-stitch beadwork. (a) The needle is inserted on the open side of the bead row. (b) The needle emerges on the groove side of the bead rows. Observing this sequence of stitching in and out helps to bead a smooth surface.*

Fig. 5-8. *Checker-board designs as on this pipe bag are a typical hallmark of the Northern Plains beading style which was shared by the Blackfeet, Assiniboine, or the Plains Cree and Plains Ojibwa (Burke Museum, Seattle; photograph by Bill Holm).*

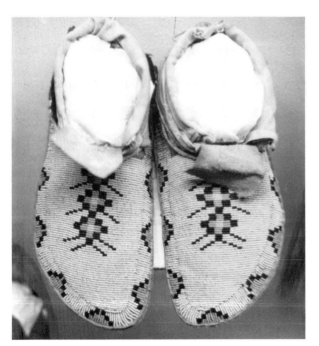

Fig. 5-9. *Pair of fully-beaded moccasins from the Northern Plains, probably Assiniboine or Blackfeet (Ian M. West collection).*

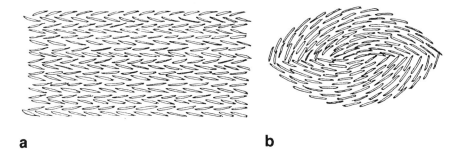

a **b**

Fig. 5-10. *On the backside, the tacking-stitches form a herringbone pattern. (a) Geometric beading with straight bead rows. (b) Floral beadwork with curvilinear bead rows.*

This method has still another advantage: you don't have to count the beads as you would have to when doing lane-stitch work; instead, you simply judge the length needed visually.

For the rest of the many rows to be beaded, your stitches may be a little bit longer and may allow for three or four beads between them, because the subsequent rows lean against the first one which was meticulously executed. The desired smoothness of your beadwork will tell how many beads it will tolerate between individual stitches.

Even if you are totally absorbed by the tacking or sewing job, you should pause once in a while to check the quality of your work. This is a good time to turn over the beaded piece and take a look at the *herringbone* pattern that more-or-less regularly builds up with each row (Fig. 5-10). This pattern is a characteristic trait of most overlay work, whichever tribe produced it. It may be straight as in geometric work, or curved as in floral work.

FLORAL DESIGNS

Most if not all tribes who beaded their floral designs in the overlay-stitch—the subarctic Athapaskan or the Creek and Seminole of the southeastern Woodland, for example—first beaded the leaf and petal outlines before they filled up the solid space; foliate scroll designs of the Alaskan Tlingit even consist of double or triple

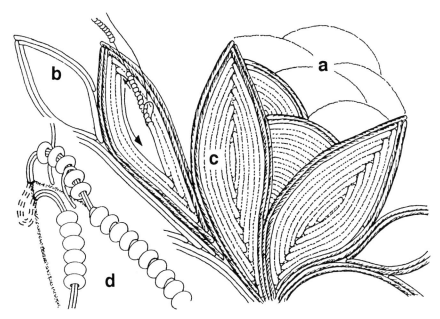

Fig. 5-11. *Beading a floral design element is dictated by the shape of petals or leaves but usually they are beaded from the perimeters to the center. (a) First draw the guidelines.(b) Bead the outlines. (c) Fill the shape with concentric rows, working in counterclockwise direction. (d) Handling the ends of bead rows in sharp corners.*

outlines only. Most beading traditions, however, would call for solidly-filled shapes, and it is here that the most varied tribal and regional differences show up.

Before going to sketch some of the better known floral styles, you should familiarize yourself with one or two basics of floral beading. Take a simple leaf with two pointed ends, for example. Start drawing the outlines first, which would make two "first rows" meeting at the pointed ends. (Remember what I said about the first row earlier!) Bead one of these "first" rows until you reach one pointed end; with the bead-thread's needle go all the way through the leather and back to the surface again. This double stitching makes the two row-ends about neatly (Fig. 5-11d). Bead the other "first" row along the line and to the point where the first row started. Again stitch through the leather and return to the surface so you can start the second row. With a stylized basswood leaf, for instance, you would have only one sharp corner or pointed end, which starts and ends one first row or outline .

To fill the shape confined now by the outlines, you should bead row after row, alternatingly on one side, then on the other. You will soon notice that the rows's ends will stagger in the two corners, with the rows themselves becoming shorter with each concentric course. Most often the gap left over by the last pair of rows allows for a short single row only, to complete the leaf.

Do not regard this instruction, though, as a fixed rule. It should only show you how to approach a floral element which also depends on the style chosen! Typical floral design traits of the Middle West and Southern Plains tribes—Mesquakie, Iowa, Kansa, Oto-Missouria, Kiowa, and Comanche for example—are abstractly-shaped and arbitrarily-colored petals with double outlines (COOLEY H 1985). Their filling-rows cross or run along the shape's main axis, or even traverse it diagonally, and therefore are fairly easy to do. On the other hand, you will find intricate rendi-

Fig. 5-12. *Umatilla woman's legging with stylized floral designs, beaded on red stroud cloth (Holm collection; photograph by Bill Holm).*

tions of flowers, sometimes beaded so realistically that you could name them by their common or scientific names, as on Ojibwa bandolier bags or Plateau women's bags popular in the early decades of this century. These styles would require careful planning and analysis.

Background areas of floral beadwork were treated in different ways, too, depending on style and region. The classic floral embroidery of the Crow, or Métis, for example, displays blossoms, leaves and stems on unbeaded foundation material (woolen cloth or leather), integrating its color and texture into the work. Most groups preferred to cover the background completely with beads, manipulating the course of the bead rows in different ways. On an Ojibwa bandolier bag, the bead rows may run straight in horizontal

Fig. 5-13. *Blackfeet moccasins beaded with floral designs (Author's collection).*

Fig. 5-14. Contour beaded *background on a Plateau handbag: the bead rows follow the contours of stems, petals and leaves (Burke Museum, Seattle; photograph by Bill Holm).*

lines, while Columbia Plateau-style floral beadwork most often made use of *contour beading* which was very popular in that region (Fig. 5-14); the bead rows, in ever-increasing arches, continue around the flower or animal shapes until these arches encounter those of further design elements (GOGOL H 1985).

I would have to write another book if I were to give detailed instructions for each of the floral styles. I urge you to compare authentic pieces, study the forms, shapes, and positions of the design elements; even examine individual bead rows and the use of colors. A given style was meant to be recognized as such by the beholder, though perhaps not exactly in the way that non-Indians conceive "style." A man's suit of black velvet covered with sparkling, richly-colored flowers and graciously curved tendrils clearly carries the message of being made by an Ojibwa woman. Stylized tulip petals, growing symmetrically from long thin stems on a little boy's buckskin jacket, may show the attention of a loving Crow mother who beaded them.

6
CROW-STITCH

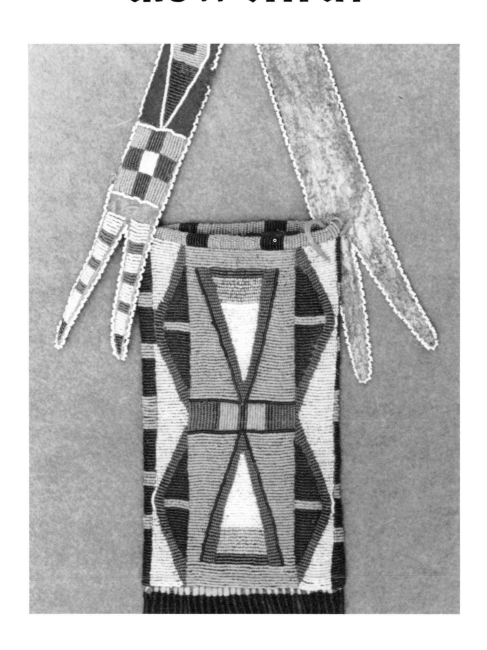

For many decades, only a few dedicated students of American Indian material culture cared about the classic beadwork of the Crow Indians. They had to rely on Lowie's classic *Crow Indian Art*, a short paper full of misconceptions (F 1922), followed 37 years later by a special issue of the *American Indian Hobbyist*, and *Crow Indian Beadwork*, an introductory study based on the notes of William Wildschut, a Montana businessman who collected for the Museum of the American Indian among the Crow. Suddenly, in the 1970's and 1980's, Crow Indian Art was in vogue among collectors and brought together scholars at a symposium to discuss controversial issues of Crow art. The *American Indian Art Magazine* published a special Crow issue (Winter 1980), and art lovers even found parallels to Constructivist paintings like those of the Dutch artist Piet Mondrian.

Among most Crow art aficionados the idea was accepted, even heatedly defended, that only the Crow made beadwork in that particular style and traded surplus clothing or accoutrements to the tribes west of the Rocky Mountains. Kindled by this widespread attention, it is only natural that the tribe's beadwork was re-evaluated in a voluminous doctoral dissertation (LOEB *F* 1983), which cast doubt on a cherished myth and placed this art into a larger context: though her view may not be shared by all scholars, the author convincingly outlined the distribution of the "Crow" style among the various tribes of the Columbia Plateau, substantiating it by historic photographs and Crow or Nez Perce oral tradition. As a consequence, her introduction of *Intermontane* style as a new name surely does more justice to the Plateau tribes, than dismissal of their geometric beadwork as being inferior imitations or "imports" would have done before. The term "Intermontane," however, has been replaced meanwhile by the more appropriate *Transmontane* which, to be consistent with current usage, will be used in this chapter as it includes the tribes on both sides of the Rocky Mountains who shared the style (LOEB *F* 1991:201).

Although this is a book more about techniques than styles, a few words seem in order to understand the nature of the Crow-stitch a little better; both its name and technique have been subject to misinterpretation like no other beading technique. It was first described in 1937 by Frederic Douglas in an analysis of a Crow horse collar, though without being given a special name. Two decades later, John C. Ewers, the editor of *Crow Indian Beadwork*, offered the names "modified lazy-stitch" or "Crow-stitch" (WILDSCHUT, EWERS *F* 1959:40). While the first term did not catch on (although it was more precise!), the latter has been with us to this day. At the time of its publication it was not fully realized how widespread the use of the Crow-stitch was. Much of the Plateau beadwork as well as that of some other Northern Plains tribes was beaded that way; you even would find this technique on the rosettes of some blanket strips beaded by the Sioux, once the Crows' arch enemies. The technique perhaps was derived from *bird-quillwork* where the stripped quills of gull feathers some-times were sewn down in a similar fashion (FEDER *C* 1987). As far as tribal attribution is concerned, "Crow-stitch" certainly may be a misnomer; but it must be conceded that, at the same time, it is a handy term, with no pejorative undertones, and perhaps for these reasons it has been established so firmly in the literature.

Although the Crow-stitch is one of the easiest beading me-thods, it is sometimes misinterpreted (MERITT *F* 1988:47), or even confused with the overlay-stitch (DYCK *F* 1988:9). "How-to" instruc-tions usually limit themselves to a single illustration of the basic principle accompanied by a few words; even advanced bead-workers confess to me that they have grappled with the exigencies of the Crow-stitch. This lengthy chapter may appear to belie my statement a few lines above; however, as in real life, many things are much easier done than explained. The chief question is not how to *do* the Crow-stitch, but how to *use* it! Once you have understood the Crow-stitch's fundamentals, you should have no more difficulties arriving at pleasing results.

TECHNIQUES USED IN TRANSMONTANE BEADWORK

PLAINS VS. TRANSMONTANE BEADING. As has been discussed in the previous chapters, the individual beads in Sioux or Cheyenne lane-beaded pieces, or the overlay-stitched geometric motifs, to some degree resemble the little boxes in a graph paper. Ignoring representational and floral beadwork, a design gradually builds up by changing the bead colors while the surface texture is maintained throughout the beadwork.

Classic Transmontane beadwork approaches the primary designs in a much different way: they were beaded as separate units. Where these designs meet with the background, slight "dips" break the monotony of a smooth surface and are further accented by the characteristic single row outlines. The *Fort Berthold* tribes

 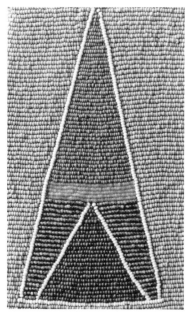

Fig. 6-1. *Comparing diagonal lines in Sioux-style beadwork and Crow-style beadwork. Left: Lane-stitch beadwork allows only a limited number of the diagonals (Beadwork by the author). Right: In Transmontane beadwork, diagonal outlines can be beaded at any angle desired (Beadwork by the author).*

(Mandan, Hidatsa, and Arikara) also beaded long, narrow triangles and diamonds as separate fields which assured oblique borders as straight as possible with the transversing bead rows fitting snugly into them. These relief-like breaks in the surface can be felt with the fingertips. Though today most craftspeople of the Crow or Nez Perce prefer a perfectly smooth surface in their work, some traditional beadworkers might reject this development by saying, "It looks like it was made in Japan!" (LOEB F 1983:83)

In contrast to the Sioux, Cheyenne, or Blackfeet women, who had to consider some technical limitations when doing geometric lane-stitch or overlay-stitch work, the Crow women had full control of their designs and could work diagonal lines at any angle desired or prescribed by tradition (Fig. 6-1). Transmontane beadwork surely has a distinct relationship with parfleche painting which often shows through; on rawhide parfleches the primary designs were surrounded by dark blue outlines, while single rows of white

Fig. 6-2. *Comparing outlines on rawhide painting and on beadwork. Left: In rawhide painting, designs most often were framed by blue outlines (Burke Museum, Seattle; photograph by Bill Holm). Right: In Transmontane beadwork, single bead-rows often outlined the primary designs (Beadwork by the author).*

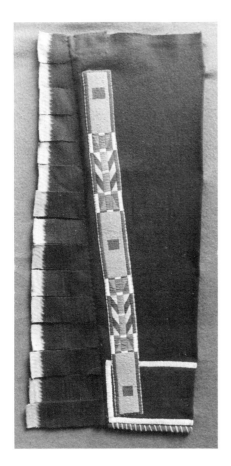

Fig. 6-3. *Crow-style strip leggings, made of stroud cloth. These design panels as well as the borders are beaded with the lane-stitch while the background areas are done in the Crow-stitch. (Beadwork by the author).*

beads outlined beaded primary designs (Fig. 6-2). The remaining work was "merely" filling in with colors and more designs.

Correspondingly, most geometric beadwork of the Northern and Central Plains can be compared with basketry, weaving, or even knitting, because the designs and the background simultaneously develop during the work; diagonal lines can only be executed at certain angles. In Transmontane beadwork this integration of the designs and backgrounds is found only in lane designs, in small figures within larger primary designs, or those floating on the background.

SEVERAL TECHNIQUES COMBINED.   Combining several beading techniques on the same article is another hallmark of Transmontane beadwork; in the classic period (1870-1910) it was a rare piece that used one technique only, such as on lane- or overlay-stitched women's leggings (Fig. 6-16), a few saddle blankets tabs, or some lance case flaps beaded with lanes only.

As a rule, all pieces display at least three different methods: *Crow-* or *overlay*-stitch for the designs and background, *overlay*-stitch for the white (or colored) outlines, and *lane*-stitch for the border and central lanes. For decorating borders and edges a third technique—*edge beading*—was widely used. (The various types of beaded edges will be discussed at length in Chapter 7).

Unlike the lane-stitch or the overlay-stitch which often was the only major technique among the beadworkers of a given tribe, the Crow-stitch must not be seen in isolation: it almost always goes together with other beading techniques. Despite its name, this stitch is a very unreliable trait when trying to attribute an object by the technique used. Do not equate "Crow-stitch" with "Crow beadwork;" I have often seen beadwork made by the Crow in the classic style which features no Crow-stitching at all!

I have come to perceive Transmontane beadwork as "shaped colors," in contrast to the "colored figures" dominating Central and Northern Plains beadwork. This independent handling of separate fields enabled the Transmontane beadworkers to use a speedier technique than the overlay-stitch to cover the fields with beads, without losing their flat surfaces.

DRAWING AND BEADING THE OUTLINES

This combined use of several techniques in Transmontane style requires a different approach to the construction of an article in that style. The perimeters and the border lanes (the center lane also, if desired) are drawn first, followed by the outlines for the primary designs (such as diamonds, hourglasses, or tall, slender triangles). Sometimes the primary designs were surrounded by tapering frames, often beaded with dark blue beads; since these frames very often are separate lanes, they should be pre-drawn, too. Smaller, or secondary designs often need marking points only for reference. Wherever you can get along without guiding lines, you should leave them out (Fig. 6-9a).

When drawing all the necessary lines, you should not be preoccupied with perfect alignment or symmetry as would be required of a draftsman. Besides the right color combinations, it is the slight irregularities that lend an authentic touch to Transmontane beadwork. In the horse-collar panel shown in Fig. 6-4 the right diamond leans toward the center lane, and the triangle in the bottom lane does not abut the left diamond's point.

There seems to be some controversy about the sequence of the individual steps in Transmontane beading; because most, if not all, researchers who visited the Crow Reservation in the 1880's or 1890's did not care to watch the women doing beadwork, we can only speculate how they proceeded. Probably you'd be correct if you beaded the outlines first and then filled the spaces thus delineated. The obtuse angles in your designs would come out

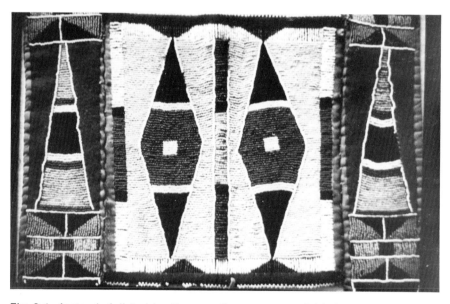

Fig. 6-4. *Instead of disturbing the overall appearance of this horse collar's panel design, the asymmetrically shaped diamonds lend an air of artistic nonchalance which is far from slipshod work (Linden-Museum, Stuttgart, Germany).*

Fig. 6-5. *Outlines may be beaded first, followed by filling out the areas with beads, or the design elements may be beaded before being surrounded by single-row outlines, as suggested by the outline's rounded corner on this Nez Perce boy's shirt (Honnen collection).*

sharply defined. On the other hand, many broad triangles feature rounded apexes and hourglasses may have slightly rounded waists, so you could likewise start with beading the body of the design first—if rounded corners are desired—and then continue by doing the overlay outlines, followed by beading the adjacent area(s) (Fig. 6-5).

BASIC TECHNIQUE

SEWING ON THE BEAD ROWS. As this beading technique's other name, "modified lane-stitch," already implies, the Crow-stitch basically is a variant of the lane-stitch, sharing with the overlay-stitch the use of tacking-threads. In a typical lane, as found in Sioux or Cheyenne beadwork, the individual rows usually have a length of roughly eight or nine beads; to fill a field of a given size, one lane is beaded next to the other (Fig. 6-6 left). A Crow-stitch "lane" uses much longer rows, depending on the width of the area to be covered (Fig. 6-6 right). While shirt or legging strips may ask for a "lane" 2 to 2 1/4 in. (5 to 6 cm) wide, panels on shoulder strips of bandolier bags often feature bead rows as long as 6 in. (15 cm). Crow-stitch "lanes" also may taper on one or both sides, as they often do between or inside diamonds, triangles, or hourglasses.

 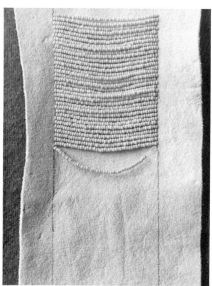

Fig. 6-6. *Crow-stitch compared with lane-stitch. Left: A typical Central Plains legging strip composed of several lanes (Ian M. West collection). Right: One wide lane for a Crow-style legging or shirt strip before being tacked down.*

FIXING THE BEAD ROWS.   Naturally, bead rows of that length will sag by the sheer weight of the glass beads and they need to be additionally fixed to achieve a smooth surface. After one panel has been fully covered between its perimeters or outlines, the bead rows are sewn down in a backstitch fashion, using a series of threads which run at a right angle to the bead rows, and, as in the previous chapter on the overlay-stitch, should be called *tacking-threads*.

The tacking-thread advances *two* rows *below* the beads and *beneath* the leather's surface, and returns *one* row *above* the beads. By starting the following backstitch, the tacking-thread forms a loop around the bead-thread which, when pulled taut, fixes the beads to the leather (Fig. 6-7). One "advantage" over the overlay-stitch is that the backstitches need not be drawn completely through the leather and back. Rather, as with the lane-stitch, they merely pass just under the surface of the leather. With most of the bison gone by the end of the 19th century, the Crow

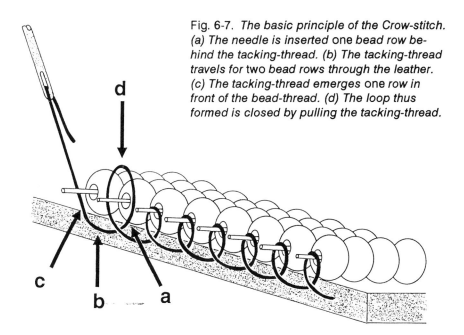

Fig. 6-7. *The basic principle of the Crow-stitch. (a) The needle is inserted one bead row behind the tacking-thread. (b) The tacking-thread travels for two bead rows through the leather. (c) The tacking-thread emerges one row in front of the bead-thread. (d) The loop thus formed is closed by pulling the tacking-thread.*

women were forced to bead many of their horse trappings on canvas. Because this material was not suited to passing the needle just under the surface, it was necessary to stitch all the way through. For a change, you may resort to canvas if only to experience a different material (Fig. 6-13), but you will soon return to well-tanned deer, elk or moose hide to do your Crow-style beadwork on: it simply works better.

Fasten the first tacking-thread five to six beads away from one border and next to the first row with a few backstitches; or sew its end to the reverse side and emerge with your needle between the first and the second rows. Now you are ready to make the first run of sewing down all the bead rows. After you have finished this first "tacking line," sew down the thread on the front or reverse side with a few backstitches and cut it off.

To avoid ripples in the rows which might result in a lane-stitch effect, you should pull the tacking-thread only as much as you *feel that the thread has emerged completely.* Depending on the width of your beadwork you may have to sew down many more tacking-threads. Although it is possible to choose a wider distance be-

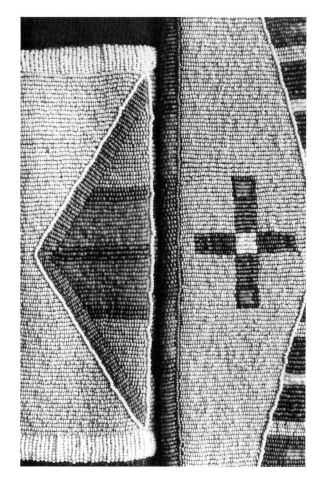

Fig. 6-8. *The smooth surface of the gun case muzzle-sleeve on the left belies the actual use of the Crow-stitch. The mirror bag on the right was beaded with the over-lay-stitch (Beadwork by the author).*

tween the individual tacking-threads and it was often done, I would recommend not to leave more than five or six beads between the threads—at least as long as you are not yet completely familiar with this beading technique. After you have gained sufficient control and done a number of Crow-stitched pieces, you may try to leave more beads between the tacking threads and still achieve a smooth surface. Ideally, when you look at an excellent piece of Transmontane-style beadwork, you should not be able to tell if it was beaded in Crow-stitch or overlay-stitch (Fig. 6-8). In both cases a surface as smooth as possible is the chief goal. On many

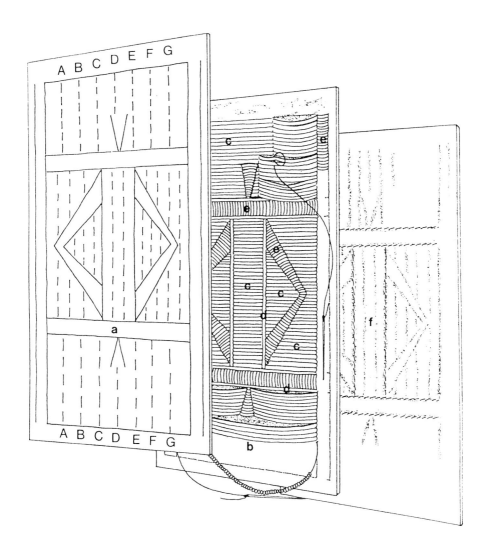

Fig. 6-9. *The various steps of Crow-stitch beading. (a) Drawing guidelines (the dotted lines—denoting the course of the tacking-threads—are, of course, not drawn). (b) Attaching the long bead rows in lane-stitch fashion. (c) Areas already beaded with the Crow-stitch technique. (d) Overlay-stitch outlines. (e) Lane-stitched lanes. (f) The reverse side of this blanket-strip panel shows the furrows created by the Crow- and lane-stitch, as well as the tacking-threads of the overlay-stitched outlines. The small triangles are also lane-stitched.*

old pieces of Crow beadwork I had to inspect the backside of the piece to see if the Crow-stitch was employed.

The sequence of sewing the tacking-threads is crucial to the quality of the final product. Rather than securing the middle of the rows first and then again in-between, I would recommend starting at one end of the rows and work your way to the other end; i.e., from "A" to "G" (Fig. 6-9a). With each subsequent tacking-thread, the bead rows lose some of their slack and tighten up. Possible "shadows" (hard to explain but when you do your first piece of Crow-stitch you will discover what I mean) created by the first tacking-thread(s) on the bead surface disappear with each tacking-thread that follows.

You may inspect the reverse side of your work, and, depending on the angle of the lighting, you will notice furrow-like dips. These dips or compressions are caused by the repeated pulling of the tacking-threads. Because most original overlay work displays the tacking-threads on the reverse side in a herringbone texture, these characteristic dips or furrows fairly well indicate the use of the Crow-stitch (Fig. 6-9f).

HANDLING LARGE SOLID PANELS

Some objects, such as Plateau-style bandolier bags, have very large panels which often are 5 to 6 in. (12.5 to 15 cm) wide and are solidly beaded, containing no design elements to interrupt them (Fig. 6-10). Beading these large fields can cause a serious problem when it comes to sewing down the tacking-threads. The farther away you get from an outer edge, the more difficult it becomes to perform the backstitch. As with all sewing techniques, you have to clasp the piece with the thumb and index finger of your left hand where you insert the needle for the backstitch. Instead of tacking down from one side to the other, bead one half and start sewing down the tacking-threads from the middle, working to the outside (Fig. 6-11a). With the first half tacked down, turn the piece around, bead the other half and sew down the tacking-threads (Fig. 6-11b).

Fig. 6-10. *Large, solidly colored panels on the shoulder straps are an outstanding feature of Plateau bandolier bags (Honnen collection).*

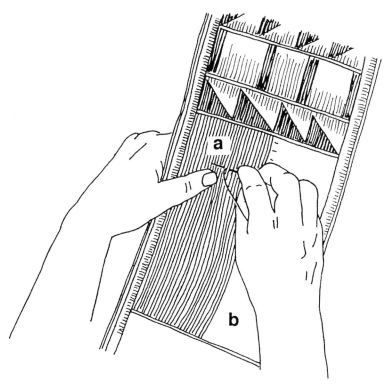

Fig. 6-11. *Large areas of a solid color like this panel on a Plateau-style bandolier bag should be "divided" into two fields. (a) First bead and tack down one half, starting from the middle. (b) Turn around, bead and tack down the other half. Carefully done, this method will not show on the finished piece but will make your beading easier.*

Though on most objects, bead rows can be tacked down from one end to the other, some, such as the panels on bandoliers, cradle tops or center panels of horse collars, should be planned well ahead with such problems in mind. As soon as you have decided on the designs and their arrangement, you should determine a beading sequence that is most convenient and allows you to find perimeters to hold the whole piece with your hands. "Perimeters" should not be taken as an absolute—any leather still unbeaded which surrounds the already beaded part can be a perimeter and thus be folded over to reach the sewing area comfortably.

BEADING LARGE ROSETTES

For a long time, Transmontane-style blanket strips have been associated with the Crow, but recent research has rather convincingly proven that most of them should be attributed to the Plateau tribes (LOEB F 1984:17,25). Large rosettes alternate with rectangular panels which were beaded in a more-or-less prescribed arrangement. Very often these rosettes contained two wedge-shaped figures forming sort of an hourglass around a circular cloth patch in the center. Between these shapes, the background was filled with concentric rows of pony or seed beads or a combination of both. While seed-beaded rosettes usually feature red triangular cloth patches in the corners, making the rosette panels nearly square, pony-beaded rosettes conspicuously lack the red corner triangles and most often are cut out along the outer boundary (LOEB F 1983:173-174). Even if the overlay-stitch is ideally suited for sewing down curved bead rows, I have seen quite a number of blanket-strip rosettes beaded in the Crow-stitch, with the the tacking-threads radiating outwards from the bull's-eye in the center.

My own experience in beading these rosettes, however, has shown that using a different approach helps overcoming a serious problem: when sewing down the bead rows of the circular segments, they have a strong tendency to turn toward the center and they never will lie flat. To prevent this, you *have to tack down each bead row individually*; i.e., a bead row is fastened and then immediately tacked down with the tacking-threads already prepared. The more you come to the outer perimeter of the rosette, the more tacking threads you'll have to work with.

Although the old-time beadworkers may have used a different approach to bead those giant rosettes, the following beading sequence should make it rather easy to bead them.

- If desired, bead the overlay outlines of the bull's-eye and the wedge shapes (Fig. 6-12a).

- Bead one circular segment as described before—by tacking down each row before doing the next one in the same way (Fig. 6-12b). Do the same for the other half of the rosette (Fig. 6-12c).

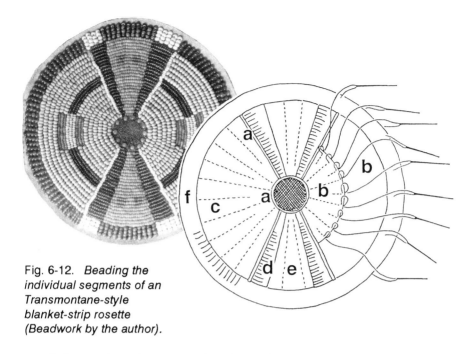

Fig. 6-12. *Beading the individual segments of an Transmontane-style blanket-strip rosette (Beadwork by the author).*

- If the wedges have tapering frame borders, bead them using the lane-stitch (Fig. 6-12d).

- Fill the remainder with beads and use the Crow-stitch (Fig. 6-12e).

- Bead the border lane, using the lane-stitch (Fig. 6-12f). Many rosettes, however, have their outlines beaded with the Crow-stitch, too.

- Of course, you may bead the wedges first, and then the background segments; but it seems that the length of the wedges is easier to control than the circular segments, so I bead the latter first.

CROW-STITCH VERSUS OVERLAY-STITCH

You should not be deceived by the technique's apparent ease: after you have fastened all or a major part of the bead rows in the lane-stitch manner, you may already get a feeling of what the item will look like. Sewing down, however, backstitch after backstitch after backstitch can take many long hours! As overlay-stitching is even much more time-consuming, you might wonder if completing an ambitious Blackfeet-style project such as a wide stole with huge rosettes could be speeded up by using the Crow-stitch. The Blackfeet craftswomen knew very well which beading technique was best suited to their style, and its neatly aligned checkerboard or stepped-triangle designs almost screamed for being beaded with the overlay-stitch.

Unfortunately, in Transmontane-style beadwork, there is no hard and fast rule which tells when the Crow-stitch and when the overlay-stitch was used. It depended solely on the individual beadworker's skill and predilections (LOEB F 1983:78). I have been amazed by this arbitrary use of different techniques on many pieces of Crow beadwork, without finding a sound reason for it. As an example, on a horse-collar (Fig. 6-13) the solidly colored background is worked in both the overlay- and Crow-stitch while you might expect it to be done in the latter technique only. Perhaps

Fig. 6-13. *The reverse side of a horse-collar panel shows the arbitrary use of the Crow- and overlay-stitch on the same item. Which technique was used depended solely on the bead-worker herself (Linden-Museum, Stuttgart, Germany).*

Fig. 6-14. *This beautiful Crow saddle-flap features most traits of classic Trans-montane beadwork: division of the main area into several fields which were beaded separately, using the Crow-stitch; white single-row outlines; border lanes; edge-beading along the cloth-bound edges; and small triangles appending from the main beaded panel (Honnen collection).*

this horse-collar was intended to be fully done in the overlay-stitch; the Crow woman beading it may have misjudged her time available because she wanted it to have finished for some relative's wedding festivities so she resorted to the quicker Crow-stitch; who knows?

ORIENTATION OF BEAD ROWS

The bead rows almost always parallelled the short side of a beaded area; or, if you prefer, they crossed its longer axis. In Transmontane beadwork the bead rows played a much more important role than would appear at first glance; they intensify the general effect and help to counterbalance elongated designs and panels. By beading designs and backgrounds separately the Crow women broke up the monotony of a smooth surface of bead rows.

In addition, bead rows crossing the long axis of diamonds, hourglasses, and tall, slender triangles abut these figures' oblique sides much better than if they ran along the axis, thus fitting snugly into the single-row outlines. If the beadworker had filled such designs with longitudinal rows, these would stretch the figure

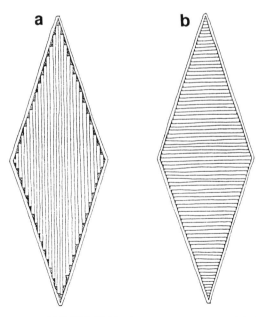

Fig. 6-15. Another fine detail in Transmontane beadwork is often over-looked. (a) If the bead-worker had filled the dia-mond with longitudinal rows, they'd stretch the figure optically and would leave staggered gaps where the rows meet the outlines. (b) Transversally beaded rows counter-balance primary designs and fit snugly into the single-row outlines.

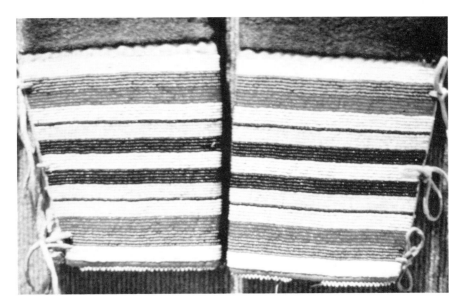

Fig. 6-16. *Overlay-beaded leggings of the Crow women with multiple stripe designs appear to defy the rule of bead rows paralleling the shorter side of a field. But wrapped around the legs they fit this canon perfectly—the Crow beadworkers were keenly aware of such subtleties and used them skilfully (Honnen collection).*

optically and leave staggered gaps along the outlines (Fig. 6-15).

Some objects, like women's leggings beaded with horizontal stripes in overlay-stitch, appear to depart from this rule. However, when the leggings are wrapped around the leg—the way they should be viewed— the principle is restored again, and the visible part of the rows is shorter than the longitudinal axis of the leggings (Fig. 6-16).

Still today, this delicately-balanced interplay of designs, organization of space, and bead rows is carefully observed by the Crow, even if their beadwork style has completely changed, and the pieces today are beaded exclusively in the overlay technique. At the annual Crow Fair the male dancers wear beaded belts, belt pouches, cuffs, and modern versions of the classic mirror bags, along with the typically flat roaches, the long Central Plains-style hairpipe breastplates, and the feathered back bustles. When these beaded costume parts are worn, their bead-rows run vertically and thus seem to emphasize the body axis of the dancers.

7
EDGE-BEADING

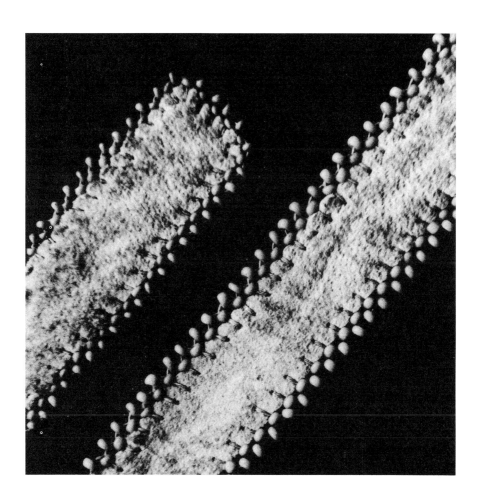

Next to the overlay-stitch, edge-beading was one of the most widely used beading techniques. Most tribes knew of various types and used them to embellish edges and borders: the Athapaskan and Tlingit in Alaska, the Crow and the Nez Perce on both sides of the Rocky Mountains, the Comanche and Kiowa of the Southern Plains, or the Iroquois of the Northeast Woodlands. Although these edge-stitches were frequently used by the Central Plains tribes (Sioux, Cheyenne, and Arapaho), those peoples favored a different technique to decorate edges which blended perfectly with their bold lane-stitch beadwork and has become known as "rolled edging." In the classic period, the Crow and the Plateau tribes did most of their beadwork with the small seed beads but they edge-beaded many of their red or dark blue cloth bindings with the larger pony beads.

Of course, you could come up with any variations of edge-beading possible as they seem to be endless; but most of those fanciful bead edges were not very common in old-time beadwork, so your research will tell you which types of edge-beading your pattern tribe used and which colors they preferred for them. While most edge-beading was done with white beads, other light colors, such as light blue, yellow, or pink, were also frequently used, and on some edges the upright beads had a different color.

If you are right-handed you should begin edge-beading at the left end, while left-handed beadworkers work from the right to the left end of the edge, so you don't have to switch the needle from one hand to the other. No matter which type of edge-beading you are going to do, start by passing the needle through the material just below the edge and return it between the doubled bead-thread, pulling it all its way through and tightening the resulting girth hitch.

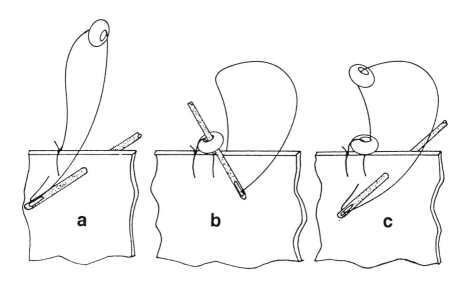

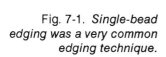

Fig. 7-1. *Single-bead edging was a very common edging technique.*

SINGLE-BEAD EDGING

After taking up one bead, pass the needle from the front side through the material—1/8 in. (0.2 to 0.3 cm) below the edge and about one bead away from the initial hitch (Fig. 7-1a). Pull the thread all the way through, return with the needle through the bead *from below*, and again pull the remainder of the thread, tugging it additionally (Fig. 7-1b). I recommend holding the bead with the fingers of your other hand while pulling the thread through the bead. To continue, take up the next bead and follow the procedure outlined above (Fig. 7-1c).

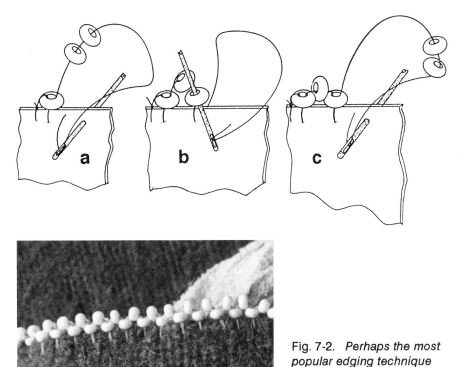

Fig. 7-2. *Perhaps the most popular edging technique was "zipper-edging."*

"ZIPPER" EDGING

This variant, probably the most common one found on old bead-work, begins like the single-bead edging by sewing down one bead (Fig. 7-1a). Then take up *two* beads, and again, pass the thread below the edge through the leather or cloth and pull it tight (Fig. 7-2a). Return the needle through the second (lower) bead, and pull the thread tight again (Fig. 7-2b). This tightening will make the other bead stand up vertically, creating a "zipper" appearance. After a number of stitches, you will develop a feeling for the correct distance between the individual stitches which depends on the size of the beads. From now on, always take up *two* beads and sew them down as described, until you have finished the edge (Fig. 7-2c).

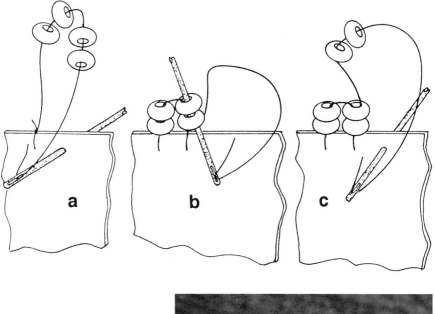

Fig. 7-3. *In Transmontane beadwork, stacked edging was often used to embellish cloth-bound borders.*

STACKED EDGING

For this edging variant, which was very popular among the Transmontane beadworkers, take up *four* beads for the first stitch (Fig. 7-3a), insert the needle at a distance of one bead and pull through all of the thread. Return the needle through the *last* two beads and pull the thread tight (Fig. 7-3b). This procedure forms two "stacks" (hence the term "stacked edging") which will be lying next to each other. For the succeeding stitches, only *two* beads are taken up (Fig. 7-3c), and the thread is run back through both of them.

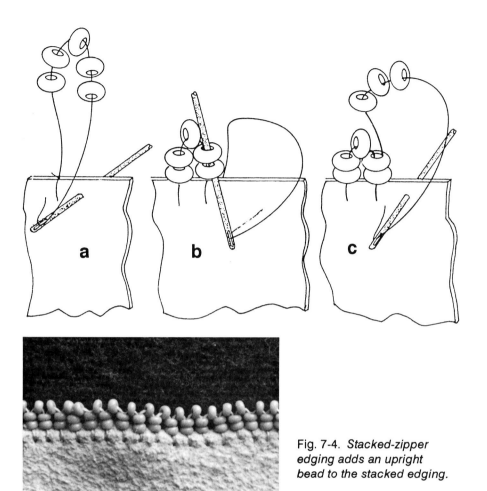

a b c

Fig. 7-4. *Stacked-zipper edging adds an upright bead to the stacked edging.*

STACKED-ZIPPER EDGING

Basically, this version follows the stacked edging with two beads stacked on each other, with the only difference that, for the first stitch, *five* beads are taken up (Fig. 7-4a), while for the succeeding stitches, only *three* beads are taken up (Fig. 7-4c). By returning the needle through the last *two* beads only, however, the third bead will automatically stand up after pulling the thread through the beads (Fig. 7-4b).

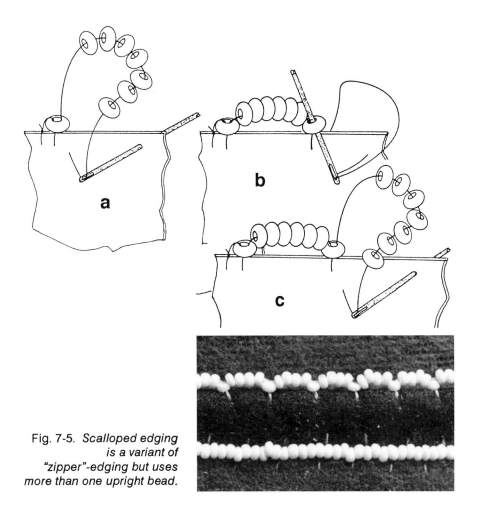

Fig. 7-5. *Scalloped edging is a variant of "zipper"-edging but uses more than one upright bead.*

SCALLOPED EDGING

While the scalloped edge is started with one bead as the single-bead and the zipper edge (Fig.7-5a), it offers some variations in the number of beads taken up—between two to eight beads—which determines the length of the rows containing upright beads. The return-stitch always goes through the last bead of the row(Fig. 7-5b), and, depending on the distance between the stitches, the rows with the upright beads can be straight or arched (Fig. 7-5c).

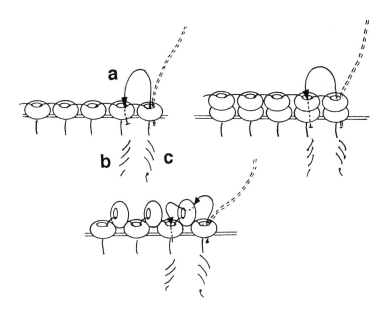

Fig. 7-6. *Starting a new thread in edge-beading. (a) The end of the thread used up passes back through the bead next to it. (b) Stitches of the old thread sewn down. (c) Stitches of the new thread which is represented by a dotted line.*

LENGTH OF WORKING THREAD

My experience has shown that a good working length of doubled thread is five times the length of the border to be decorated. As we remember, however, this working thread should not be longer than 30 in. (75 cm), which, with seed beads, will produce a beaded edge of about 6 in. (15 cm). Before the thread is used up, at least 4 in. (10 cm) of thread should remain for sewing down. Instead of taking up new beads, stitch back through the last bead lying flat (Fig. 7-6a), and, with a few backstitches, sew the thread below the edge on the backside of the leather or cloth (Fig. 7-6b). At the same place start a new thread and pass it from below through the last bead (or beads, depending on the type of edge you are using) worked in; you are then ready to continue edge-beading (Fig. 7-6c).

ROLLED EDGING

Mouths of pipe bags, quivers, and bow cases, or the lateral edges of Crow mirror bags, just to name a few examples, were beaded in a technique which to some degree resembles the overcast-stitch and also bears some relationship to the lane-stitch. Before starting rolled edging, draw a guide-line on the outside and fold over the edge of the leather to form a bulge or roll. To create an even edge and to ease the actual beading, you even may sew this bulge with a few running-stitches so that its edge on the inside of the mouth aligns more-or-less with the pre-drawn line. Fasten the bead-thread on the inside.

As you would do with the lane-stitch take up the needed number of beads, and, from the front side, stitch the needle on or just below the pre-drawn line through the leather, emerging on the inside. Hold the bead row firmly with your other hand while you pull the thread taut. Unlike lane-stitch beading, in rolled edging

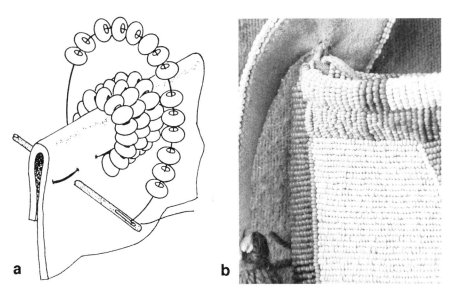

Fig. 7-7. Rolled edging. (a) This type of edging is best done on an edge of the leather folded over and sewn down with a few running stitches. (b) On Crow mirror bags, edges were most often finished with rolled edging (Beadwork by the author).

you always insert the needle from the outside and emerge with it toward the inside of the object (Fig. 7-7a).

It takes some practice and experimentation to know the proper length of a bead row in order to accomplish a tight rolled edge. No matter how carefully you do this, the bead rows seldom will be as tight as in regular lane-stitch beading. Because it is quite difficult to align the stitches on the inside perfectly to each other, this effect should not disturb you too much—original beadwork quite often shows that the old-time beadworkers had to tackle this problem, too.

8
WOVEN BEADWORK

Very likely, among the tribes of the Upper and Western Great Lakes region, woven beadwork evolved from the delicate woven quillwork as well as fiber-twining which, for many generations, had been made by these groups. The Ojibwa, Menominee, Potawatomi, and the Winnebago, as well as many other tribes of the Northern Woodlands and the Eastern Prairies or Midwest have been known for weaving many objects such as bandolier bags, garters, sashes, or hair ties, and by the middle of the 19th century, woven beadwork was in full blossom among these peoples.

We can only guess that, in this early period of woven beadwork, the women tried various methods of weaving, adopting some while abandoning others, until they arrived at results satisfying to them. They saw that their weaving endeavors turned into serviceable objects, adding beauty to their traditional clothing.

The magnificent bandolier bags—noted for their wide range of colors as well as for their diagonally and vertically oriented designs—are typical examples of the Winnebago who seemed to prefer the *loose-warp* weaving technique but also used the *cross-weave* method. The Ojibwa, on the other hand, did most of their loom-work with the *standard-weave* and only a few pieces known from this tribe were done with techniques known as *heddle-loom weaving* and *diagonal* or bias weaving (LESSARD *H* 1986:68).

Along with delicate and complex geometric designs—for which bead weaving seemed to be predestined—floral designs played a large role in woven beadwork. Although bead weaving did not easily lend itself to perfectly-rounded shapes, these limitations challenged the beadworkers to experiment with the designs, and, eventually, come up with a new floral style which was quite different from embroidered floral beadwork. The elaborate geometric designs, however, which are found so frequently in woven beadwork, clearly refute the common notion that strictly associates Woodland beadwork with floral designs and Plains beadwork with geometric designs. Toward the end of the 19th century, overlay-stitched floral beadwork quickly superseded woven beadwork.

For too long, native bead-weaving, which only recently received an attention that was long overdue, had been dismissed by some authors as kitsch and even was said to be a White man's invention (POWERS D 1986:138), taught to Indian children in school. Paradoxically, at the same time loomwork has been over-emphasized by many Indian crafts books which, however, limit themselves to the standard technique and claim it to be the most "comfortable" or "easiest" beading technique. Any beadworker who has seriously attempted the various techniques will readily agree that the lane-stitch or Crow-stitch, for example, are much easier to do than weaving beads with any of the techniques described in this chapter.

Before going into the details of bead-weaving, some important terms should be introduced here, with more terms following later when they will be needed.

- *Warp* is the passive element fixed between two points, although in loose-warp weaving and diagonal-weaving it can be quite "active." To differentiate the individual strands in a warp, I will call them *warp-strands* (Fig. 8-1a) .

- *Weft* is the active element, running forth and back across the warps and creating the fabric. Again, for better differentiation, I will call this the *weft-thread* (Fig. 8-1b).

- *Loom* is a device holding the warp-strands stretched taut.

As in other weaving techniques, we find two major principles in bead-weaving:

- In most bead-weaving techniques the warp-strands are enclosed by the weft-threads (Fig. 8-1c), while in heddle-loom weaving the weft-threads are enclosed by the warp-strands (Fig. 8-1d).

- Taut warp-strands are stretched firmly on a box or tension loom which I will call *fixed-warp weaving*, versus loose warp-strands fastened at one end only which, correspondingly, should be called *loose-warp weaving.*

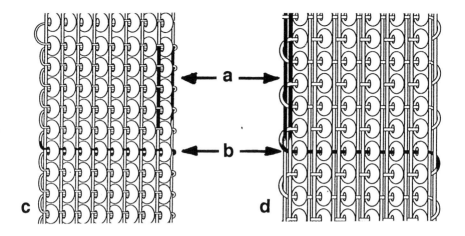

Fig. 8-1. *Terms and features used in woven beadwork. (a) Warp-strands. (b) Weft-threads. (c) In most weaving techniques the warp-strands are enclosed by the weft-threads. (d) In heddle-loom weaving the weft-threads are enclosed by the* warp-strands.

Firm warp-strands, quite a bit stronger than the weft-thread, should be used—I work with heavy-duty #12 size cotton thread satisfactorily, and old pieces seen in museums sometimes feature warp-strands even twice as thick as the wefts. Beads as uniform as possible are a must if you want to arrive at good results.

LOOMS

Much fixed-warp weaving was done on a *tension-loom* (Fig. 8-2c), which enabled even the longest warp-strands to be spaced evenly and stretched taut. The far end was fastened to a convenient point such as a small tree or a nail on the wall, while the near end was tied to the weaver's belt—by bending forward or leaning back the weaver was always able to control the tension on the warp. You will have to add a foot or two to the actual length of the warp-strands to allow for the *spacing bars* at both ends. These spacing bars are just wooden slats, with a series of holes drilled into them. You might even do very well without such holes and simply wind

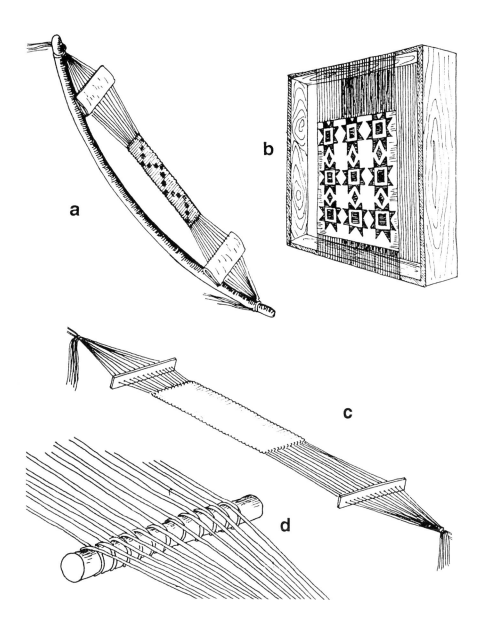

Fig. 8-2. *Various types of looms. (a) Bow loom with birch-bark spacers. (b) Wooden box-frame loom with the warp wound continuously around it. (A heddle loom is shown in Fig. 8-8). (c) Fixed-warp weaving—tension loom with spacing bars. (d) Instead of drilling holes into the spacing bars simply wrap the warp-strands around them.*

the warp-strands evenly around dowels (Fig. 8-2d). Smaller objects may be woven on a rigid loom such as the bow loom (Fig. 8-2a), while the wooden box-frame loom allowed for longer pieces and probably was used quite commonly (Fig. 8-2b). Although I strongly recommend to do your weaving on a tension loom because it is very easy to construct as well as light and compact enough to transport to any place, you might want to consult such books as *Crafts of the North American Indians* for detailed instructions on various types of useful looms (SCHNEIDER *B* 1972:143–149).

STANDARD-WEAVE

After you have warped a loom with the required number of well-waxed warp-strands which is one more than the number of beads woven across, tie a *single* well-waxed weft-thread (with a needle threaded at its other end) either to the very left or right edge warp-strand (Fig. 8-3a). Before starting the actual weaving, the first three or four passes of the weft-thread should be made *without* beads to reinforce this end of your piece. Alternatingly go with the needle over and under the warp-strands—be sure that after the very last of these preliminary passes the weft-thread comes out *above* the edge warp (Fig. 8-3b). When stringing the beads onto the weft-thread, you will of course not forget to observe the sequence of colors dictated by your chosen design for each

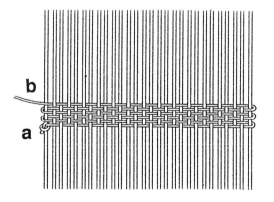

Fig. 8-3. *Starting standard-weave loomwork.*
(a) A single weft-thread is tied to one of the outermost warp-strands.
(b) For a few passes, the weft-thread is woven under and over the warp-strands without beads—care should be taken that the weft-thread is on top of the warp-strand after the last pass.

row—if this is your first attempt at bead weaving, you should start with a simple design so you can concentrate on the technique alone.

With the beads strung on the weft-thread, place it *under* the warp-strands and push the beads against them with your index finger, spacing them evenly between the warp-strands (Fig. 8-4a). You will learn immediately that spacing the beads often turns out to be a tricky job which slows down your work considerably and

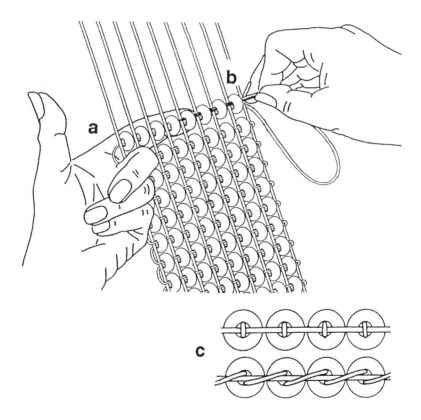

Fig. 8-4. *Basic elements of the standard-weave. (a) After spacing the beads between the warp-strands they are pressed against the warp with the index-finger. (b) The needle returns on top of the warp to secure the beads. (c) On one selvage the weft-thread returns through the bead while on the other it proceeds to the next row.*

belies the alleged ease of woven beadwork. To secure the beads between the warp-strands, return the weft-thread through the beads, but this time *on top* of the warp-strands (Fig. 8-4b). All you have to do now is the sequence just described: stringing the various colors of beads on the weft-thread as required by your design; spacing them between the warp-strands; and anchoring the beads by returning through them with the weft-thread. If, after a few passes, you look at both selvages of your weaving, you will notice that on one the weft-thread makes a right-angled turn, while at the other it advances to the next row at an oblique angle (Fig. 8-4c). Finish your piece with a few over-and-under passes without beads as you did at the start, tie off the weft-thread and cut the piece from the loom. Depending on the article you have woven—garters or sashes—you can interweave the free ends of the warp-strands with colored wool yarns to form long braided tassels. By the way, this finish can be used with any of the weaving techniques when long tassels are needed for tying or decoration.

CROSS-WEAVE

At first glance, the cross-weave technique shows no difference from the standard-weave: the texture of the finished piece looks the same, and the weft-threads pass through the bead holes both above and below the warp-strands. The major differences, however, are the use of *two* weft-threads and *two* needles as well as the way the weft-threads turn around the edge warp-strands.

First, tie both (single!) weft-threads to one of the edge warp-strands, and with both of them weave a few passes without beads to reinforce the beginning of your piece; take care that both weft-threads come out at the same edge warp-strand. String the desired color sequence of beads on the weft-thread that exits *above* the edge warp-strand and place it *below* the warp-strands; while pressing the beads up with your index finger, space them evenly between the warp-strands (Fig. 8-5a). *Above* the warp-strands, go through the beads with the needle of the *other* weft-thread, at the same time taking care that your needle does not pierce any of the warp-strands (Fig. 8-5b). On wide pieces your

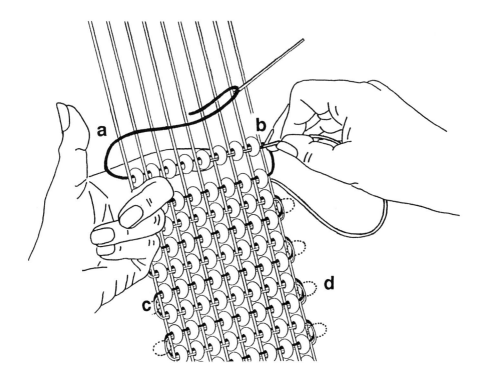

Fig. 8-5. *The cross-weave uses two weft-threads. (a) The first weft-thread which carries the beads is pressed against the warp. (b) The second weft-thread passes on top of the warp through the beads to anchor them. (c) The alternating function of both weft-threads causes "crosses" on the selvages. (d) An extra bead can be strung which covers the crossing of the weft-threads.*

index finger will not be long enough to push all of the beads against the warp-strands, so you will have to repeat this job several times until it exits the last bead on the opposite edge.

To string the beads for the second row, use the weft-thread that *anchored* the beads of the first row, then place it below the warp-strands. With the weft-thread that *carried* the beads of the previous row run through the beads of the second row.

After a few rows, you will clearly see the pattern of the cross-weave technique: both weft-threads change their function after each row from "bead-thread" to "anchoring-thread" and vice versa, with the bead-thread running *below* the warp-strands and the anchoring-thread *above* the warp-strands. In other words, you can use the thread you just have pulled through the beads and still keep it in your hand to string the beads for the next row.

Each time you start a new row the weft-threads cross automatically on the edge warp-strands and form an "X," which explains the name "cross-weave" (Fig. 8-5c). If you wish, these crossings of the two weft-threads allow you to create a decorative "zipper edge" by stringing as many beads as you have warp-strands on your loom: one bead will always cover the crossings of the weft-threads and thus protect them from abrasion (Fig. 8-5d). After having completed your weaving, do not forget to weave a few passes *without* beads to secure the warp-strands at this end, too.

WEAVING FRINGE TABS

Bandolier bags were frequently decorated on the bottom edge with a row of "fringes" or tabs which ended either straight across or in points, and usually were woven with the same technique that was used for the pouch itself. Because each tab was woven individually after dividing the warp-strands into smaller units, weaving tabs of equal width requires careful planning of the object's total width. If you should decide to add tabs long after you've started weaving, it will be extremely difficult to arrive at the desired amount of equally wide tabs.

Decide on the number of tabs you want to have on your article. Each tab should preferably have an odd number of beads across, allowing for the design to be centered nicely on the tab. Multiply both numbers (tabs and beads across each tab) and add the number of tabs minus one. Continuing with the example of the bandolier bag, let's assume 11 tabs which is a number commonly found on such bags: multiplying these by 19 beads of one tab which is an average width for tabs makes 209; by adding 10 beads for the one-bead gaps between the tabs, we will have a total width of 219 beads for the bag. This example, by the way, has the odd number of beads needed in loose-warp weaving explained later. You really have to do some calculations to achieve a carefully balanced layout, depending on the design(s) you want to weave.

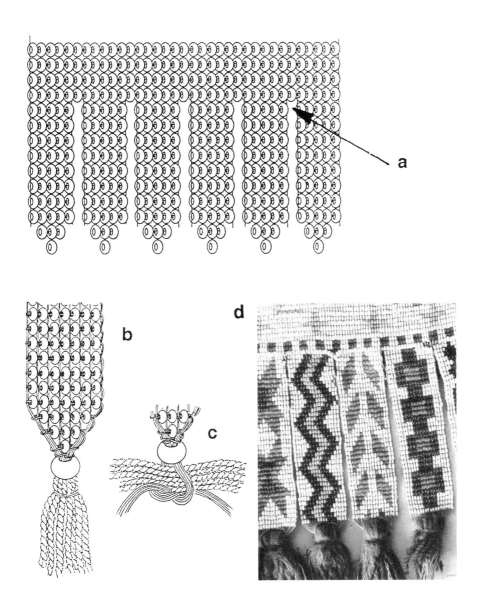

Fig. 8-6. *Weaving fringe-tabs for bandolier bags. (a) Because there is a gap of one bead between each tab, the number of beads across the bag has to be established before you start weaving. (b) A common method to weave the points of the tabs. (c) Adding tassels to the tabs. (d) Fringe-tabs on an Ojibwa bandolier bag (Museum für Völkerkunde, Freiburg, Germany).*

To weave points, with each subsequent row, string two beads less and catch the free warp-strands into the weft-threads until you arrive at the last row which may consist of one or two beads, depending on the number of beads you started your tab with (Fig. 8-6b). The remaining bundle of warp-strands was usually tied off, or drawn through a large necklace bead and tied around a tassel of colored wool yarn or silk ribbons, which may have been wrapped with colored silk thread (Fig. 8-6c). Sometimes pointed tabs were truncated, ending with a row of four or five beads and allowing for fuller tassels, or they were even woven with two pointed ends and finished with two tassels. Study photographs of typical bandolier bags to learn about other variations of tab decorations.

HEDDLE-LOOM WEAVE

Although both the standard-weave and the cross-weave have been commonly classified as "weaving" techniques, there is another method of weaving beads that shares two basic features with true weaving:

- The *heddle*, a comb-like device, which creates a triangular opening or *shed* between the two sets of warp-strands which run through its holes and slits.

- As a consequence, the warp-strands enclose or even conceal the weft-threads.

Though not quite authentic, you might try to build a special loom for heddle-weaving as suggested in a craft article (LOTTER *B* 1973), but as a rule, classic heddle-weaving was limited to narrow objects such as sashes, hair bands, and garters. These probably were woven not on a frame loom, but rather on long warp-strands which were simply suspended between two fixed posts, or tied to the weaver's belt with one of their ends. It has been said that using a heddle-loom cuts the weaving time into half because there is no need to make another pass through each weft; this may well be true but I don't think that saving time is the right approach to Indian-style beadwork. If it will take six months to weave a bandolier

Fig. 8-7. *Garter woven with the heddle-loom (Burke Museum, Seattle; photograph by Bill Holm).*

bag with the *loose-warp* technique, then you have to work six months on this project to make it look authentic—very soon you will regret having wasted three months on beadwork done in the wrong way!

HEDDLE.   Basically, a heddle consists of a number of narrow slats with tiny holes drilled in their centers and mounted between two wooden bars. I will not go into the details of the construction but the illustrations and some imagination should help you to construct a heddle of wood (Fig. 8-8a); make the heddle wide enough so you can use it for different projects. As with the spacing bars, the distance between the holes and the slits does not have to correspond to the tiny seed beads exactly. Most heddles were carved out of wood and sometimes had handles on the top bar carved in simple animal or ornamental shapes. These wooden heddles often closely resemble those brought into the country by Scandinavian immigrants, and it seems quite possible that the Indian bead-

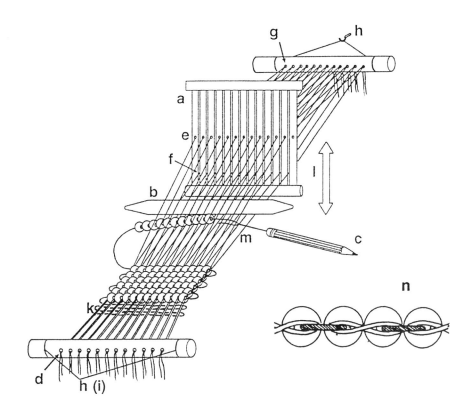

Fig. 8-8. *Heddle-loom weave. (a) Heddle. (b) "Warp separator rod" or "shed stick". (c) Pencil with eraser which "lengthens" the needle while weaving. (d) Hole in spacing bar. (e) Hole in heddle slat. (f) Slit between the slats. (g) Hole in the other spacing bar. (h & i) Fixing points for the warp-strands. (k) Preliminary passes without beads before actual weaving. (l) Raising or lowering the heddle to open the sheds alternatingly. (m) Pulling the warp-strand with the beads through the shed. (n) Typical heddle-weaving selvage.*

workers adopted these tools as well as the heddle-weaving technique for their own use (HOBBS *H* 1989:42).

OTHER TOOLS. One secret of successful heddle-loom weaving is a "shed stick" or "warp separator rod" which simply consists of a wooden dowel, about the width of a broom stick and longer than the width of your beadwork (Fig. 8-8b). Also, though not really

"Indian," a pencil with an eraser at its other end may be very helpful when doing wide pieces of heddle-woven beadwork (Fig. 8-8c).

WARPING THE LOOM. White warp-strands are very likely to show too much between the beads, so you might use medium brown thread instead (or white thread stained in a tea solution) which blends better with the bead colors and is less conspicuous. On the other hand, colored yarns were quite often used as warp-strands to add color to garters or arm bands and to provide fringes at their ends. To space the beads comfortably between the warp-strands, the shed must be wide open, requiring warp-strands much longer than the actual object's final length.

As *two* warp-strands will be needed for each bead, thread two of them through the first hole on the left side of one of the spacing bars or wrap them around the bars if you don't want to drill holes (Fig. 8-8d); you even might omit the spacing bars altogether because the heddle helps spacing the warp-strands evenly. Pull one of this pair through the hole in the middle of the heddle's first slat (Fig. 8-8e), while its mate is pulled through the next slit to the right (Fig. 8-8f). This done, thread both warp-strands through the first hole of the other spacing bar (Fig. 8-8g). Repeat this procedure with all the double warp-strands required for your project, and tie the warp-strands—stretched taut—between two convenient points (Fig. 8-8h). Tying one spacing bar to your belt helps you to maintain a constant tension on the warps (Fig. 8-8i), and to roll up the finished part which may be necessary on a long piece of loomwork.

WEAVING WITH THE HEDDLE LOOM. Knot the weft-thread to one of the edge warp-strands, raise the heddle and insert the warp separator rod into the shed (Fig. 8-8b). You will notice that the function of the warp separator rod is to keep the shed open, thus making it unnecessary to hold the heddle in position as you weave. Pass the weft-thread *without* beads from one side to the other through the shed and remove the rod; lower the heddle, insert the rod, and make the next pass, again without beads. Do this for several more times, as this preliminary weave keeps the warp-strands from unravelling when the piece will be removed from the loom (Fig. 8-8k) Push the weft-threads close together to make a tight weave, but do *not* pull on the wefts, otherwise the warp-strands might get too close to each other and leave not enough space for the beads.

String the required number and color sequence of beads; to "lengthen" the needle, stick it, after stringing the beads, into the eraser of the pencil (Fig. 8-8c). Depending on its previous position, raise or lower the heddle (Fig. 8-8l), and, after placing the rod into the shed to keep it open, with the pencil pull the beads through the shed (Fig. 8-8m). For the first few rows, spacing the beads between the warp-strands will be a tricky job, but soon you will get the hang of it. Remove the rod, lower the heddle and place the rod into the new shed; string new beads and stick the needle into the eraser to weave the next row. After each pass, move the heddle towards the bead row to push it against the previous one, thus making a tight weave. At the same time take care to keep an even tension—but not too much!—on the warp-strands as well as on the weft-threads.

LOOSE-WARP WEAVE

A weaving technique which was very popular among the Winnebago departs radically from fixed-warp weaving and is called *loose-warp weaving*: as its name implies, it is done with warp-strands mounted at one end while their other ends hang free; weaving is done from top to bottom (whereas in fixed-warp weaving work usually proceeds from bottom to top, or away from the weaver's body); the warp-strands are the *active* elements or, in other words, those one works with primarily. Another important feature of loose-warp weaving is the complete absence of a loom—all you need basically are beads, threads, a needle, and a pillow. Long thumbnails will help to split the double wefts easily.

STARTING YOUR WORK. To prepare the "starting cord" (LANFORD H 1984:32), pull a thread half-way through a needle, make two knots about a quarter inch (0.5 cm) apart from each other at the

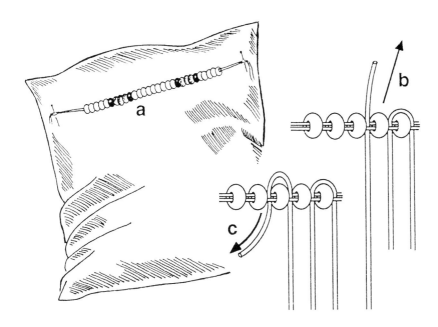

Fig. 8-9. *Preparing loose-warp weaving. (a) Beads strung on a "starting cord" which consists of a doubled thread with a pair of knots at each end and which, after adding all of the warp-strands, is pinned to a pillow. (b) Inserting a weft-thread between the starting cord. (c) Pulling the weft-thread over a bead and back between the starting cord.*

end of the doubled thread and string the required number of beads which should be an *odd* one (Fig. 8-9a).

Cut the warp-strands at least *twice* the length of your bead-work; for comfortable work at the bottom, however, you should add some 10 inches (25 cm) which will be trimmed off when your work is finished. Size #12 cotton thread is ideal for the warp-strands. To find the number of warp-strands needed, add "1" to the number of beads strung on the starting cord and divide the sum by two: in our previous example with the fringe tabs (do not forget the tabs if you want to have them!), we had calculated a bag proper 219 beads wide, so divide 220 by 2 which will give you 110 single warp-strands: doubled they will make 220 warp-strands again.

To the right of the first bead on the right end of the bead row, split the doubled thread with your thumbnail, and, from below, insert the first warp and pull it halfway through (Fig. 8-9b). Push a bead tightly against the warp-strand, split the thread on the other side of the bead and insert the end of the same warp-strand from above, pulling it through until its center rests on the top of the bead, allowing the ends to dangle free (Fig. 8-9c). Push the next bead against the first one, and continue by placing a warp-strand around a bead and pushing the next one against it. As I have noted before, you must string an *odd* number of beads to warp your starting cord correctly: if you used an even number, you would end up with one warp-strand missing at the other edge of your work which is needed to turn around the weft-threads. After having inserted all the warp strands, finish the starting cord with another pair of knots and fasten it with two pins to a *pillow* (Fig. 8-9a) which will be placed on your lap to work conveniently. Although this "pillow method" may not be historically correct I have used it very successfully and it will not alter the result of your weaving.

WEAVING. After having knotted the ends of a long, doubled weft-thread—which, of course, should have a needle at its far end—to the right edge warp-strand, string all the beads needed for the next row in the sequence of colors required by the design. If the length of your weft-thread permits, you may even string the beads for many more wefts; to prevent the beads from sliding down the weft-thread, secure the needle temporarily in the pillow as you will not need it for a long time. Move up a bead against the warp-strand and leave some eight inches (20 cm) of the weft-threads exposed between this bead and the bulk of the other beads (Fig. 8-11a). Split the weft-threads with your thumbnail, and with your right thumb and index finger reach between the weft-threads (Fig. 8-11b); grasp the next warp-strand and pull it back between the weft-threads (Fig. 8-11c). Move another bead against the warp-strand just worked in, again split the weft-thread and pull the next warp-strand through, and so forth until the row has been finished. While working at it, you will almost automatically press the beads with your fingers against the previous row. Also, from

Fig. 8-10. *Bandolier bags with elaborate design arrangements were a hallmark of Great Lakes woven beadwork (Burke Museum, Seattle; photograph by Bill Holm).*

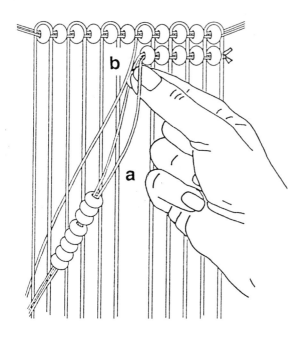

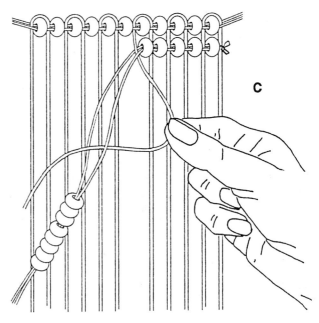

Fig. 8-11. *Basic steps in loose-warp weaving.*
(a) *After a bead has been moved against the warp-strand, the weft-thread should be exposed for a couple of inches.*
(b) *Index and middle finger reach between the weft-threads and grasp the next warp-strand.*
(c) *The warp-strand is pulled back between the weft-threads. Pushing up the next beads starts this cycle again.*

time to time pull on the weft-threads to pack the beads tightly together, but you should take care not to pull *too* much.

CROSSING WEFT-THREADS AT SELVAGES.   Having woven the first row completely, both weft-threads emerge from the last bead, one in front of and the other behind the left edge warp-strand. Remove the piece from the pillow, turn it over and pin it back to the pillow; if you haven't strung the beads for a number of wefts already, string the beads for the next row. To turn both weft-threads around the edge warp by crossing them over each other, you may use the following method: (1) from below, reach with the thumb and index finger of your *right* hand between the weft-threads—the index finger must be *in front* of the thumb and only the fingernails should touch the threads! (Fig. 8-12a)—and make a half-twist *away* from you (Fig. 8-12b); (2) after the half-twist, leave your fingers between the weft-threads and grasp the right edge warp-strand (Fig. 8-12c); (3) let the weft-threads go and pull them with your left hand around the warp-strand to the left while pulling the warp-strand with your right hand to the right (Fig. 8-12d); (4) immediately push the first bead of the next row into its place to secure the crossing of the weft-threads. By turning over the piece after each row, you can continue weaving in the same direction and do the crossing of weft-threads always with the same hand. In this fashion, continue weaving this row as well as the others until your work is completed.

The pouch of a Winnebago bandolier bag often was woven in the loose-warp technique, while its shoulder strap probably was done with the standard- or cross-weave because its very long warp-strands are more easily handled with the fixed-warp weaving techniques. Loose-warp weaving surely takes much more time to complete any larger piece of beadwork, and in our fastmoving contemporary life, this tedious technique seems to have no place. It looks tedious, and it *is*! After trying one row or two you will most likely shout, "No way!" But if you patiently stick with this work and do some more rows, you will perhaps discover that it really is not that bad. Once you have accustomed yourself to this weaving pattern, you may very likely come to enjoy the "one bead at a time"

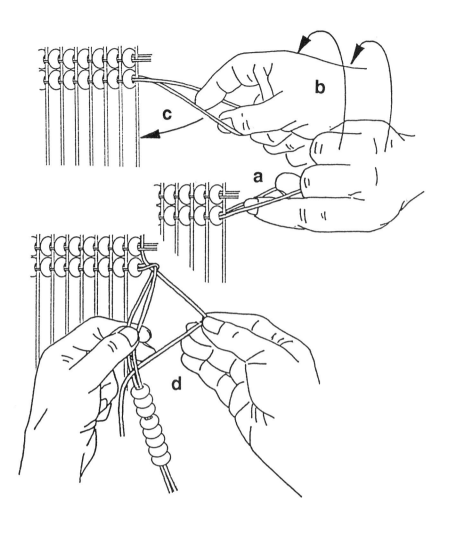

Fig. 8-12. *Crossing weft-threads at the selvage implies a "twining" movement. (a) Thumb and index finger are inserted as shown between the weft-threads. (b) The hand turns and thus crosses the weft-threads in a half-twist. (c) Still holding fingers between the weft-threads, the fingers reach for the warp-strand. (d) The warp-strand is pulled through the weft-threads, and the next bead is moved up to secure the crossing.*

rhythm it shares with the gourd-stitch—a rhythm not easily found in standard- or cross-weaving. Being related to Indian basket making as well as Chilkat weaving of the Northwest Coast as far as the manual movements are concerned, loose-warp weaving has become my favorite method among the bead-weaving techniques. As a fact, loose-warp weaving has one great advantage over fixed-warp weaving: bead rows can be pressed much closer against the previous rows, producing a tighter weave and thus a much firmer product.

DIAGONAL WEAVING

Although sharing the free-hanging warp-strands with loose-warp weaving, diagonal weaving resembles "braiding" pretty much. Anyone who has fingerwoven yarn sashes will immediately recognize the relationship between both techniques: for each pass, warp-strands change their function and become weft-threads (Fig. 8-13). Actually, this technique should not be called "weaving" at all, and textile terminology classifies it instead as "oblique interlacing."

Diagonal weaving, which is sometimes also called *bias-weaving* or *side-stitch*, was commonly used by the beadworkers of the

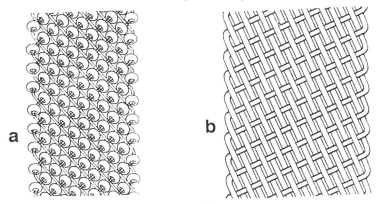

Fig. 8-13. *Technically, diagonal weaving (a) bears some relationship to finger-weaving or "oblique interlacing" (b): in both methods the weaving elements change their function from warp to weft with each pass.*

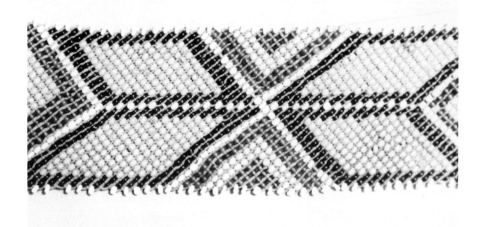

Fig. 8-14. *Chokers were often made by using the diagonal-weaving technique (Wisconsin State Historical Society; photograph by Richard Schneider).*

Great Lakes and Midwest tribes, such as the Potawatomi, Menominee, Mesquakie, or the Winnebago in order to create narrow bands. Diagonal weaving has been said to be one of the most difficult beading techniques but once you've mastered its basics, it is very easy; very likely, you will find yourself enjoying this kind of weaving, accepting its tediousness as a part of the job. You just need a lot of time to complete a choker or a hair tie.

PREPARING WARP-STRANDS. Use a strip of soft buckskin which is a little bit wider than the piece to be woven, and cut its bottom edge at an angle of roughly 45° (Fig. 8-15a). The length of the warp-strands is determined by three factors: (1) the object's length; (2) roughly 50 percent of this length should be added, accounting for the take-up in each row (Fig. 8-15c); (3) they must be doubled. As a result, cut them at least *three times* the length of the object you want to weave and cut as many warp-strands as beads to go across a row. You may have to plan their length very carefully, and, in a few cases, will end up with extremely long warp-strands. Thread *each* of them on a needle, pull it halfway through and knot the ends together. With girth hitches tie each doubled warp-strand

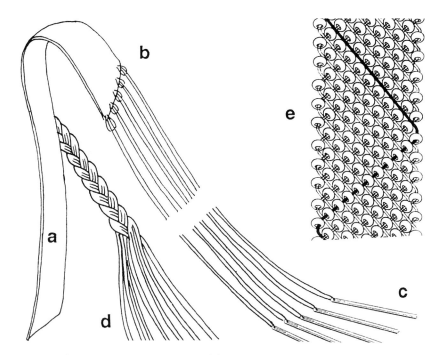

Fig. 8-15. *Starting diagonal weaving. (a) Buckskin strip cut at an angle of roughly 45°. (b) Tying the doubled warp-strands with girth hitches to the buckskin strip. (c) Needles at other end of warp-strands. (d) Starting from a braid. (e) Because of its course and double length, cut the warp-strands at least three times the total length of the object to be woven.*

to the bottom edge of the leather piece, maintaining an equal distance of a bead's width (Fig. 8-15b). With a pin fasten the leather piece to a pillow which, as in loose-warp weaving, is placed on your lap so you can work conveniently.

WEAVING.   Let's assume that you work from right to left, so the angled bottom edge of your buckskin piece should slant up to the right. On the first warp-strand on the right, string the number of beads which equals that of the doubled warp-strands. Move the first bead up to the edge of the buckskin and, with your thumbnail, split the first warp-strand between this bead and the others. Reach between with the thumb and index finger of your right hand and grasp the second warp-strand (the next one to the left) and pull it

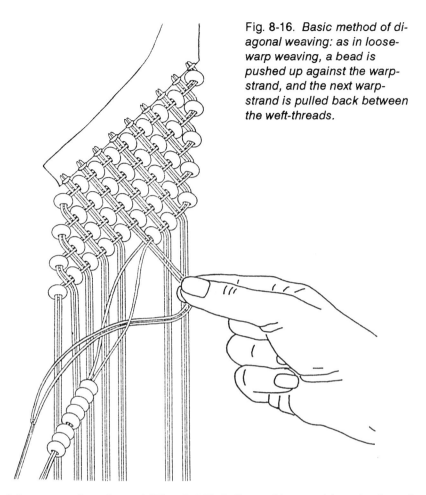

Fig. 8-16. *Basic method of diagonal weaving: as in loose-warp weaving, a bead is pushed up against the warp-strand, and the next warp-strand is pulled back between the weft-threads.*

back between first thread (Fig. 8-16), followed by pushing the bead against the bottom edge of the buckskin piece—actually, this is the same sequence as we have learned in loose-warp weaving! Push the next bead against the second warp-strand and pull the third warp-strand through first warp-strand.

Press the beads against the bottom edge of the leather piece and continue moving up a bead and pulling the next warp-strand through the first one, until all of them have been pulled through, pushing up the last bead against the last warp-strand to complete the first row. You will notice that the last bead has no warp-strand to border it on the far side and that after weaving a complete row

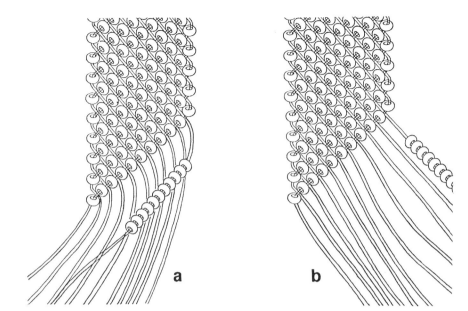

Fig. 8-17. *(a) Before weaving a row, the warp-strands should be placed to the left. (b) After completing the row, all warp-strands will be on the right side—place them to the left again to start the next row.*

all warp-strands are on the right side of your weaving. For the next row, carefully pull out the first warp-strand on the right side and leave it in this position, while you have to put the other warp-strands back to the left side (Fig. 8-17). String the beads on the far right warp-strand and repeat the steps outlined above. You will soon observe that the first and the last bead of each row automatically form a "zipper" edge.

Although waxing causes the doubled warp-strands to stick together, you should wax them well. For the first few rows, the warp-strands will very easily bundle together, and you may have a hard time to disentangle them and to prevent them from getting knotted: *very carefully* pull the warp-strand out of the bundle. Practice will come with time, and after having completed ten rows or so you will have a set of warp-strands you can handle quite easily.

To finish your strip, knot the warp-strands 5/32 in. (about 0.4 cm) away from the edge of another buckskin strip which also

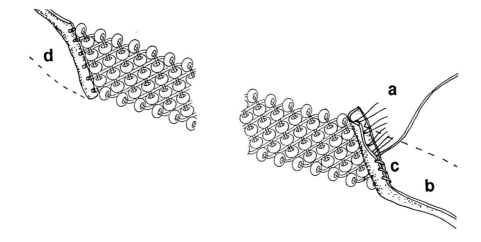

Fig. 8-18. *Finishing a diagonally woven piece. (a) Knotting the warp-strands to a second buckskin strip. (b & d) Cutting the strips into narrow thongs. (c) Sewing the second strip with an overcast-stitch.*

should be angled at 45° (Fig. 8-18a). Cut along the angled bottom edge of the leather strip—leaving a 5/16 in. (about 0.8 cm) margin—and continue cutting along the long edge of the leather strip, forming a narrow thong (Fig. 8-18b); fold over the edge around the knots and sew together with an overcast-stitch (Fig. 8-18c). Cut the first buckskin strip in similar fashion (Fig. 8-18d). On a choker, these thongs can be used to tie it around your neck.

DESIGNS. As this technique's name implies, bead rows form a diagonal axis which influences the composition of the designs. If you are not familiar with diagonal weaving, you may want to draw your designs on a graph paper designed for woven beadwork which you will find in the appendix (page 195). With pencil and ruler draw a diagonal line across the beads which will stand for one edge of the strip (Fig. 8-19a). Count the number of beads which corresponds your chosen width and draw another diagonal line, paralleling the first one and going through this "bead" (Fig. 8-19b). In the same way draw a third line in the middle of the strip (Fig. 8-19c). With colored pencils you can now draw in your designs which,

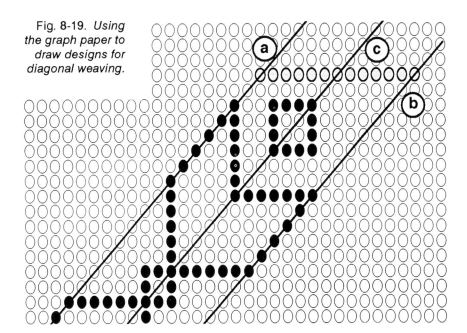

Fig. 8-19. *Using the graph paper to draw designs for diagonal weaving.*

despite the same amount of beads on both sides of the center line, will always look a bit off-balance, because of the diagonal position of the beads in the weaving. The axis formed by the *diameters* of the beads will be longer than the axis formed by their *width*—triangles covering the whole width of a strip will always have a long and a short side. Besides the slanting bead rows, this is one of the most outstanding features of diagonally woven beadwork.

I was told that some Native beadworkers string *all* beads before they start weaving. This, of course, requires a special talent for visualizing the design of the *whole* strip and, at the same time, the mental ability to break up the designs into individual rows as well as their sequence on the individual warp-strands. Using pre-drawn designs on graph papers helps to overcome these problems, although I cannot imagine that the old-time beadworkers used graph papers if they actually did diagonal weaving this way. Draw your complete design on the graph paper as described before. Assuming that your planned strip is 13 beads wide, with a pencil draw a line through the first row which should be labeled "warp #1" (Fig. 8-20). Continue this line vertically

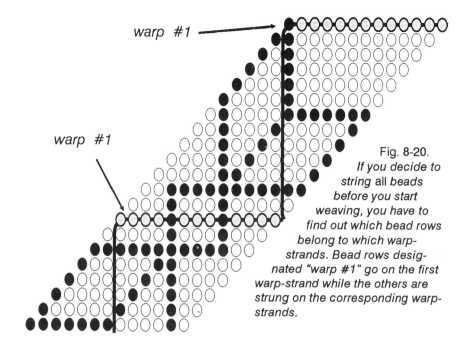

warp #1

warp #1

Fig. 8-20.
If you decide to string all beads before you start weaving, you have to find out which bead rows belong to which warp-strands. Bead rows designated "warp #1" go on the first warp-strand while the others are strung on the corresponding warp-strands.

between the beads until you arrive left of the 14th row. This row will be labeled "warp #1" again. Continue drawing this "zigzag" line until you arrive at the end of the strip, labeling every 14th line going through a bead row in the way as you did before.

Fasten the first doubled warp-strand with a girth hitch to the buckskin strip and string the beads of *all* rows that you labeled "warp #1" and knot the end of the warp-strand. Fasten the next warp-strand and string it with the beads of the next row, and so forth, until have strung all warp-strands with their corresponding beads. It should go without saying that you have to watch the color sequence of the beads very, very carefully while stringing the beads—once you discover a mistake while in the middle of weaving you have to unstring all warp-strands back to the row where you made the mistake!

As an artist and craftsman, I would feel too limited in my beadwork by stringing all the beads before I start weaving because I would have to stick to the sequence once chosen and could not make any alterations to the designs. But I have included this method which may work quite well for you, and which without doubt may have its merits.

SPLITTING INTO TRAILERS.   Among the Mesquakie of Iowa, the unmarried girls traditionally bound their hair at the back, where it was adorned with a hair binder—a rectangle of wool cloth decorated with panels of overlay beadwork at the upper and lower ends. This cloth was wrapped around the hair and held in place by a center piece of woven beadwork which was wound several times around the cloth binder; the most spectacular parts of this ornament, however, were two long beaded pendants which reached almost to the ground (TORRENCE *H* 1989:16). These unique hair ornaments were regarded as talismans and were made by the girl's relatives; at the day of her wedding she would take them off and store them at some hidden place, and even her husband was not allowed to see them again (OWEN *H* 1902:97–99).

As a rule, the center piece was woven with a heddle-loom, and the long, trailing warp-strands were plaited into a braid, or woven, at each end for some 4 in. (10 cm). From these braids, long, diagonally woven strips started, which most often were split into narrower trailers—these, in turn, sometimes were split again into still narrower trailers.

As these strips often are started with an odd number of warp-strands, one more double warp-strand is needed to start trailers of equal width, thus a strip starting with 11 beads across will split into two trailers being six beads wide each. Continue weaving the right trailer (Fig. 8-21a), but this time string only six beads for each subsequent row. After completing the right trailer, add another doubled warp-strand, next to the left edge of the finished trailer (Fig. 8-21b). Weave the left trailer, either with the same designs of the right one (Fig. 8-21c), or arrange the sequence of beads so that the left trailer's designs will mirror those of the right trailer.

A probably less common technique even results in mirroring the direction of the bead rows on the trailers, thus creating a chevron pattern when the trailers are placed side by side. To accomplish this—in the same example of a band being 11 beads

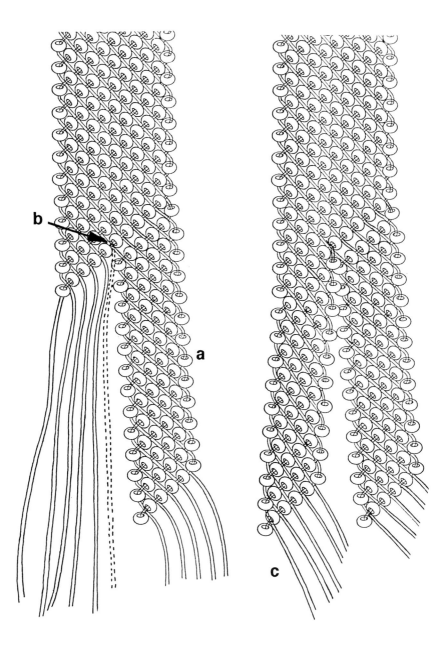

Fig. 8-21. *Probably the most common method of splitting diagonally woven pendants into trailers. (a) Weave the right trailer. (b) Next to the completed trailer knot a doubled warp-strand. (c) Weave the other trailer.*

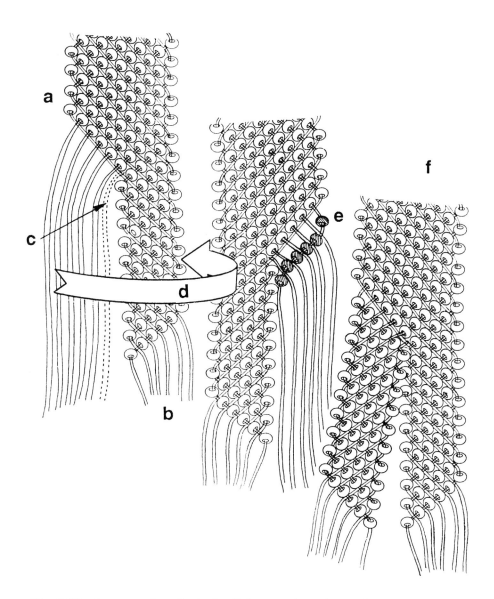

Fig. 8-22. *An unusual method of splitting pendants into trailers, observed on Mesquakie hair ties. (a) Number of beads is reduced with each subsequent row until it corresponds to the width of a trailer. (b) The right trailer is woven. (c) Next to the completed trailer a doubled warp-strand is fastened. (d) The pendant is turned over. (e) Finally the other trailer is woven. (f) Finished pendants with split trailers, showing their bead rows slanting in chevron fashion.*

Fig. 8-23. *Splitting pendants into trailers of equal width. Left: Maintaining the same direction of the bead rows, as shown in this pendant (Wisconsin State Historical Society; photograph by Richard Schneider). Right: Weaving the bead rows of the trailers at opposing angles (Beadwork by the author).*

wide—you proceed as follows: (1) Work in, as usual, the 11 beads; (2) For the next row, work in 10 beads only; (3) for the subsequent rows, work in one bead less; i.e., 9, 8, 7, and 6 beads—you will have woven a point (Fig. 8-22a); (4) continue weaving the right trailer until its end or until you want to split it again (Fig. 8-22b); (5) next to the completed trailer tie a new pair of warp-strands to the last warp-strand that goes from the strip into the trailer (Fig. 8-18c); (6) turn the strip over so you can work again from right to left (Fig. 8-22d); (7) start weaving the other trailer by stringing six beads on the first warp-strand on the *right* side; (8) pull the second warp-strand on the right side between the first warp-strand, and continue until you have worked in all of the six warp-strands (Fig. 8-22e)—you will notice that this trailer produces diagonal bead-rows at an *opposite* angle (Fig. 8-22f); (8) continue weaving until its end or to its next split which again starts with weaving a point.

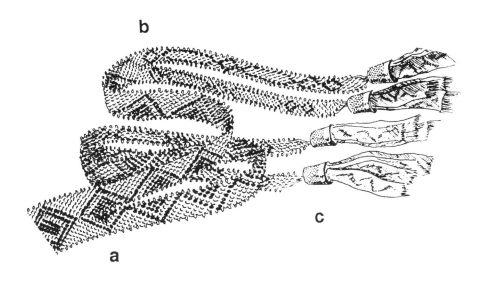

Fig. 8-24. *Pendants were usually woven with an odd number of beads across. (a) Another warp-strand has to be added at the first split. (b) Depending on the number of beads in the pendants another set of warp-strands also must be added at the second split. (c) Very often, the tips of the trailers were decorated with silk ribbons, yarn tassels and/or brass thimbles.*

On strips starting with 11,15, 19, 23, 27, 31, 35, or 39 beads (and so on) you will need an additional warp-strand at their *first*, but none at their *second* splitting. For example, if you start with a strip that is 31 warp-strands wide, you add another doubled warp-strand for the split which makes a total of 32 warp-strands (Fig. 8-24a). Each of the resulting trailers is 16 warp-strands wide which divide evenly into eight warp-strands for the subsequent trailers. Strips starting with 9, 13, 17, 21, 25, 29, 33, 37, or 41 warp-strands need additional warp-strands at *both* splittings: 34 warp-strands (i.e. 33 plus one), for example, divided by two make trailers 17 warp-strands wide—you have to add another one to come up with nine warp-strands for each of the subsequent trailers (Fig. 8-24b).

Warp-strands of finished trailers are simply tied together or braided, and decorated with tassels of wool yarn or silk ribbons, sometimes dangling from brass thimbles (Fig. 8-24c).

9
GOURD-STITCH

During a peyote ceremony, which begins at sundown and continues through the night to close with a breakfast at dawn, the participants gather inside a tipi around a crescent-shaped altar. Important paraphernalia of the ceremony are the "roadman's" or leader's staff which is said to represent a bow or lance, the fan, and gourd rattle, as well as the fans the other participants hold in their hands. These colorful and highly-ornamented instruments are covered in a very special technique which has been known by various names: *gourd-stitch*, *net beadwork*, or *peyote-stitch*. Although the latter name has been commonly used in the literature, it would be wise to follow the current usage of the term "gourd-stitch," which perhaps is derived from the gourds used for the ceremonial rattles. A further technique used to embellish the ritual objects is the Comanche-stitch, or brick-stitch, which completely differs from the classic gourd-stitch.

Despite peyote beadwork's close relationship with the *Native American Church*, gourd-stitch beading has by no means been restricted to instruments used in its ceremonies; unlikely articles such as cigarette lighters, key rings, or salt shakers, very often are decorated in this technique. Outside of Oklahoma, which seems to be the home of the most refined and elegant gourd-stitch beadwork, the Sioux of South Dakota form another center of this art. Although Indian beadwork has been traditionally women's work, the Sioux surprisingly allow the men only to do that kind of beadwork.

Once exposed to these techniques, you will understand why they attract Indian and non-Indian beadworkers alike. Unlike the other beading techniques, gourd-stitching can be an end in itself, and you may experience the repeated selection and working-in of one bead at a time as a special way of meditating.

BEADS

An outstanding feature of peyote beadwork is the use of very small and uniform beads, mostly imported from Czechoslovakia. If available from the suppliers, 13/o to 16/o beads are preferred. The smaller the size, the finer and more elegant the designs and patterns become, and my own experience has repeatedly shown that it is not difficult at all to work with 14/o beads.

Unlike old-time beadwork, in gourd-stitch beadwork any shade or hue available from the suppliers is permitted, with taste and tradition being the only limits. Sparkling *cut beads*, nowadays much sought after but expensive and hard to come by, have always been popular with the gourd-stitch beadworkers.

Combined with the various techniques, designs offer a wide range of embellishing dancing or ceremonial paraphernalia: various zigzag motifs colored with rainbow effects (frowned upon in earlier beadwork) show up frequently; feathers, pipes, even Christian symbols like crosses decorate many a staff or gourd rattle. Among the Sioux beaders, US flags seem to be a traditional holdover from their classic, lane-stitched beadwork.

TOOLS

Although this type of beading can be done with the *sharps* used in the sewn beading techniques, I would recommend long and very thin needles (#13 or #14, depending on the bead size). Normally, these fragile needles would be too fine to do any serious sewing work; but they will stand the few occasions when you have to sew down a used thread and fasten a new one.

Any fine thread —cotton or synthetic—can be used, as long as it is well waxed. For two reasons the thread should be very fine: (1) it has to fit through the narrow eye of the needle; (2) it passes twice through each bead, and three times through the last bead in a circuit before starting the next one. This multiple passing through the beads also explains why the thread is *never* doubled: the tiny holes of 14/o beads would not allow for six thicknesses if a doubled thread were used.

PREPARATIONS

Before you embark any ambitious project, you should practice on a simple wooden dowel of a half-inch (1 cm) diameter or so. The wood is covered with thin white deerskin sewn or glued in place; only conservative non-Indian beadworkers would object to gluing the leather, which is an accepted way among the Indian crafts-people. Glue a piece of leather around the dowel and cut off all excess leather (Fig. 9-1b). To make the seam as smooth and flush as possible, flatten it with a tool such as a bone-folder or the blunt back of your scissors' blade. This leather allows the beads to indent the leather, thus holding them in place; and the thread ends are also fastened into it. This same procedure applies to work beaded with the Comanche-stitch, or to bead-wrapping.

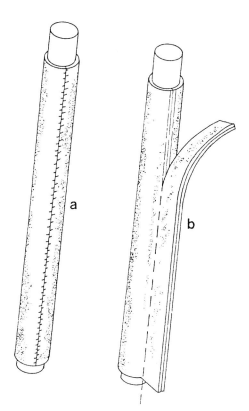

Fig. 9-1. *Covering article with leather.*
(a) Sewn around shaft with baseball-stitch.
(b) Glued around shaft, with excess leather cut off flush and seam smoothed with bone-folder.

WRAPPING BEADS

Bead-wrapping, which probably preceded the gourd-stitch, was used in older times to decorate narrow cylindrical objects with beads. Awl cases, tomahawk handles, pipe stems, drum stands, and the loops of the bead-wrapped loop necklaces (once very popular among the men of the Northern Plains tribes) are typical examples. Unless you wrap leather thongs or tightly twisted cloth strips with beads, you have to cover your object with leather to enable the bead thread to be sewn down at intervals. The number of beads to be strung before sewing down depends on the design arrangement you have decided on; I would not recommend a length of strung beads exceeding 6 to 8 in. (15 to 20 cm). While wrapping this bead thread around the object, it must be held really taut: one method is to hold the free thread end in your front teeth, with the last bead pressed tightly against them. If this does not work with you, place the thread end under a heavy weight. With the bead thread held under tension, roll the cylindrical shaft towards the end of the bead row (Fig. 9-2a). Firmly hold the last wrap in place with your other hand while you backstitch the thread

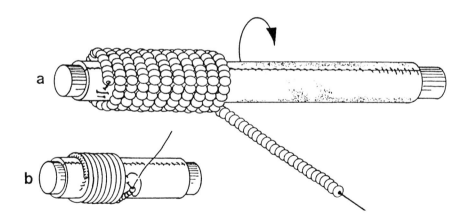

Fig. 9-2. *Wrapping beads. (a) Holding the bead thread taut while rolling the shaft toward yourself. (b) Sewing down the end of one wrapping.*

through the leather. To continue smoothly, make another pass through the last bead next to the backstitch (Fig. 9-2b). Though not absolutely necessary, even narrow bands of a different color should be sewn down before you continue with wrapping.

"UNIT-OF-THREE" PATTERN

The most commonly used technique of gourd-stitch beading is based on *units-of-three*; its principle will become clearer when you read the following instructions. The term "units-of-three" was coined by Richard E. Past in a three-part-series on American Indian net beadwork in *Powwow Trails* many years ago, which introduced me to the subtleties of the gourd-stitch (PAST B 1969). Some twenty years later this same author radically changed his approach and presented a revised edition of his superb articles (PAST B 1990). To avoid confusion, it should be stated clearly that both approaches—this book and Past's articles—arrive at the same results and are valid in their own right, although some of the various methods may be different.

DETERMINING THE NUMBER OF BEADS. As gourd-stitching is normally started at the bottom of any article and works toward the top, fasten the thread end near the lower end. To prevent the beads

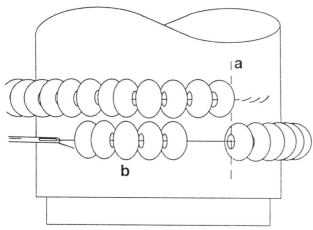

Fig. 9-3. *Finding number of beads needed for starting the gourd-stitch. (a) Line which determines the circumference. (b) Surplus beads are removed from the thread.*

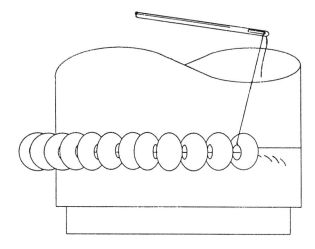

Fig. 9-4. *Wrapping beads again around shaft and pulling needle through first bead.*

from slipping off, place the starting point some 1/4 in. (0.6 cm) away from the very end. (How to cover the remaining visible leather will be detailed later.) String a number of beads (of the background color) that would go around the shaft, plus a few more and wrap this string around the shaft, aligning both ends of the bead row next to each other (Fig. 9-3). Count the number of beads that equals the exact circumference of the shaft and remove the excess beads. The number of beads remaining on the thread must be divisible by three; for example, if it ended up with 53 beads, another bead should be added to make 54. A third of the total—18 beads in this example—must then be removed and is an important step in beginning gourd-stitch beadwork. The number of the beads removed must *not* equal a *prime number* (divisible by one and itself only); if it does, you will end up with one design element larger or smaller than the rest, whether or not it is desired.

The thread containing the remaining two-thirds of beads again is wound around the shaft, with the needle passing again through the very first bead (Fig. 9-4); the way the needle passes through the bead establishes your working direction which depends on your being left-handed or right-handed. While holding the beads with the thumb of the other hand next to the very first bead, lightly pull back the thread into the opposite direction to take out any slack in the initial wrapping. You should hold the beads on the thread with your hand while working in the first four or five new beads to maintain a constant tension.

STARTING THE FIRST THREE ROWS.   A new bead is taken up, and, *skipping* the next bead of the row, the needle is passed through the following one, remembering to pull the thread taut in the same backward motion as described above (Fig. 9-5). After a few beads are added by following the sequence of taking up a new bead and skipping a bead on the row, you will quickly notice that three beads will always create a series of diagonal "steps" (Fig. 9-6), with the exception of the very first "step," which temporarily will have two beads only until you complete the first circuit. Continue in this fashion until you arrive at the last step.

To complete the first circuit after the last full "step" or diagonal series of three beads, pick up another bead *("c")* and with the needle go through bead *"a"* and through bead *"b"*; the step which had two beads while working in all the new beads now has three beads, too (Fig. 9-7). This first circuit has created *three* rows in one run, but from now on each circuit will produce only one row. The liberal use of "circuits" and "rows" should not confuse you; soon a clear distinction will be established and adhered to.

A beginner may wish to try a test piece by using beads of different colors for each row to understand the principles better. After deciding on three easily distinguishable colors, string bead

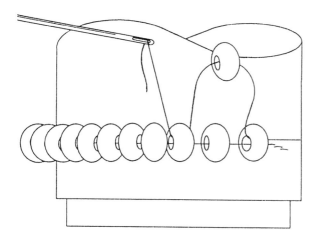

Fig. 9-5. *Working in first bead.*

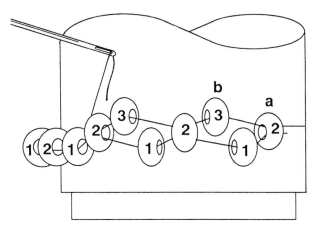

Fig. 9-6. *First three circuits are worked in one run.*

of color #1 and color #2 alternatingly until you have two-thirds of the total number of beads determined before, then start the first circuit with the individual beads as described above, using color #3 now. Each row will be of the same color, while the spirals will be multicolored.

The direction of the sloped "three-bead-steps" depends on the direction your needle travels. If you are right-handed, the needle travels to the left but the steps ascend to the right; if left-handed, the steps will ascend to the left, with the needle traveling to the

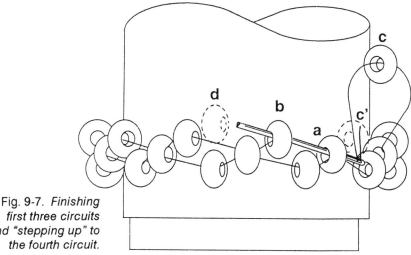

Fig. 9-7. *Finishing first three circuits and "stepping up" to the fourth circuit.*

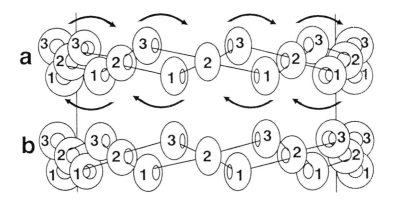

Fig. 9-8. *Transposing beads to change initial spiral direction.*

right. You may, however, reverse the direction by shifting the uppermost and the lowermost beads to their opposite side; thus, you can carry on in the direction most convenient to you (Fig. 9-8).

If you recall the number of beads you added during the first circuit in this example, you will realize that they correspond exactly to the 18 beads which you removed at the very beginning of the work; they also equal the number of the slanting steps encircling the shaft. Later, after a few more circuits, you will recognize that the beads form spirals winding diagonally around the shaft, "like the gathering of smoke that suddenly swirls upward, echoing the prayers addressed by peyotists" (COE *I* 1986:153).

Now you should take a moment to see if all "steps" align neatly and slope to the same direction; adjust any "step" which does not fit properly into the pattern. At the same time, these "steps" form the *units* necessary for the correct computation of designs which will be discussed in detail later. You will notice beads protruding on the upper edge of the work: just for reference, I will call these the "uppermost" beads. These conspicuous beads will provide some orientation: instead of skipping a bead simply pass the needle through the "uppermost" beads during the future circuits.

From now on, the process continues the same: taking up a single bead and pulling the needle through the next "uppermost" bead until the needle steps up again through bead *"a"* and bead

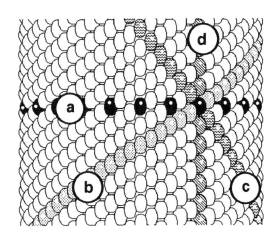

Fig. 9-9. *Special terms
used
in this chapter.
(a) Circuit.
(b) Spiral.
(c) "Counter-spiral."
(d) "Vertical line."*

"*b*" (this time of the fourth circuit), to begin the fifth circuit (Fig 9-7). This point of stepping up to the next circuit continually moves along the shaft with the direction of work as succeeding circuits are completed.

Although I have tried to avoid jargon, for a better understanding of the instructions a sort of terminology has to be introduced.

- The "circuit" we have been familiar with by now; from now on I will use this term instead of "row" as the spirals might be perceived as rows, too (Fig. 9-9a).

- The "spiral" which gradually ascends to one direction and is always diagonal (Fig. 9-9b).

- The "counter-spiral" which runs at a more-or-less right angle to the spiral (Fig. 9-9c); its implication will be discussed later in detail.

- The "vertical line" which is self-explanatory (Fig. 9-9d).

- "Pattern" is defined as the course of the spirals which adds to the appearance of the beadwork.

- "Design" is a shape or figure defined by different bead colors.

- "Design element" denotes a single element that is repeated several times around the shaft.

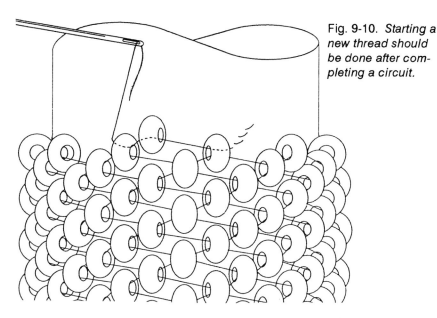

Fig. 9-10. *Starting a new thread should be done after completing a circuit.*

STARTING A NEW THREAD. No matter how long your thread has been, it will be consumed by the many circuits, leaving an end too short to work comfortably with. After completing a circuit, with a couple of backstitches this thread end is sewn down and then is cut off. Add a new thread with another series of backstitches anywhere close to the last circuit worked in. Pass the needle through an "uppermost" bead and pull the thread taut. Take up the

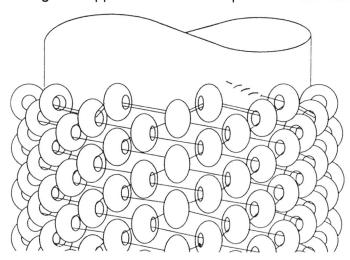

Fig. 9-11. *Finishing gourd-stitch beadwork.*

first bead of the next circuit and continue working as usual (Fig. 9-10).

Remember that a small portion of the leather was left unbeaded when you started working. If the first circuit had been started on the very edge of your fan handle or rattle, you might have had a hard time to bead it neatly, which is crucial for successful work. With your work completed, or if you prefer to do this earlier, turn your object upside down, add a new thread as described before at any convenient bead as if you had run out of thread, and bead the circuits still needed to complete this end. To finish the last circuit of your gourd-stitch work, pass the thread one or two times through the last and second-to-the-last circuits and sew it down with a few backstitches, taking care that these are not in plain view (Fig. 9-11).

DESIGN PRINCIPLES

Thus far, only the technical aspects have been discussed, mentioning some of the designs used in gourd-stitch work; you may already have learned to enjoy the steady rhythm of picking up a bead at a time and working it in. The almost total freedom in creating designs, however, perhaps is the greatest fascination gourd-stitch beadwork has to offer.

Recall the observations made when you started gourd-stitching your object or practice piece. The third of the beads removed from the thread is identical both with the number of the units or spirals which go around the shaft and the number of beads worked into any given circuit. It is these *units* which determine the number of design elements possible in an object of a given circumference. Again, be aware of prime numbers which affect the even spacing of design elements; you may have to experiment a little bit to find dowel sizes which prevent prime numbers.

To make planning of designs and understanding their principles easier, the table (page 172) contains only combinations *divisible by three*, and units representing *no* prime number. A typical width for rattles, ceremonial staffs, dance sticks, or loose-feather fan handles would roughly range between "48:16/32" and

TABLE OF UNITS & DESIGN ELEMENTS

12 : 4 / 8

D	U	S	L	O
2	2	3	5	1

18 : 6 / 12

D	U	S	L	O
2	3	4	7	2
3	2	3	5	1

24 : 8 / 16

D	U	S	L	O
2	4	5	9	3
4	2	3	5	1

27 : 9 / 18

D	U	S	L	O
3	3	4	7	2

30 : 10 / 20

D	U	S	L	O
2	5	6	11	4
5	2	3	5	1

36 : 12 / 24

D	U	S	L	O
2	6	7	13	5
3	4	5	9	3
4	3	4	7	2
6	2	3	5	1

42 : 14 / 28

D	U	S	L	O
2	7	8	15	6
7	2	3	5	1

45 : 15 / 30

D	U	S	L	O
3	5	6	11	4
5	3	4	7	2

48 : 16 / 32

D	U	S	L	O
2	8	9	17	7
4	4	5	9	3
8	2	3	5	1

54 : 18 / 36

D	U	S	L	O
2	9	10	19	8
3	6	7	13	5
6	3	4	7	2

60 : 20 / 40

D	U	S	L	O
2	10	11	21	9
4	5	6	11	4
5	4	5	9	3

63 : 21 / 42

D	U	S	L	O
3	7	8	15	6
7	3	4	7	2

66 : 22 / 44

D	U	S	L	O
2	11	12	23	10
11	2	3	5	1

72 : 14 / 58

D	U	S	L	O
2	12	13	25	11
3	8	9	17	7
4	6	7	13	5
6	4	5	9	3
8	3	4	7	2
12	2	3	5	1

75 : 25 / 50

D	U	S	L	O
5	5	6	11	4

78 : 26 / 52

D	U	S	L	O
2	13	14	27	12
13	2	3	5	1

81 : 27 / 54

D	U	S	L	O
3	9	10	19	8
9	3	4	7	2

84 : 28 / 56

D	U	S	L	O
2	14	15	29	13
4	7	8	15	6
7	4	5	9	3
14	2	3	5	1

D = Number of design elements
U = Number of units in one design element
S = Number of beads in a short side
L = Number of beads in a long side
O = Number of background beads to be added when starting design elements

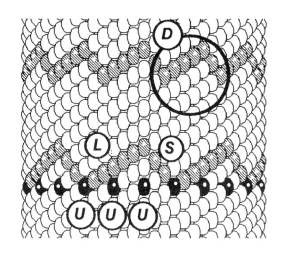

Fig. 9-12. *These parts of typical gourd-stitch designs play an important role in the buildup of designs.*
D = Design element.
L = Long side.
S = Short side.
U = Units within a design element.

"63:21/42," the first number referring to the total beads required for the circumference. The number after the colon indicates the number of beads to be removed, representing at the same time the total number of units; the number after the slash stands for the beads to start your work with. *"D"* denotes the chosen number of *D*esign elements and *"U"* the number of *U*nits contained in a single design element —the columns *"S," "L,"* and *"O"* will be explained later (Fig. 9-12).

No matter how many design elements you have chosen, or whether or not these elements are connected to each other (feather motifs come to mind), each design element begins with a single bead. If you divide the total number of units by the number of the individual design elements and subtract one bead, you will have the number of beads added between the beads of the new color worked in. These numbers are listed in the column *"O"* which stands for *"O*ld color" or the background color. This process may be better understood in the example below.

Assuming a shaft circumference of 54 beads featuring 18 units (shaded in the table on page 172), we choose light blue for the background and have a zigzag band start with six points in red. Each of these points represents a single design element *("D")*, containing three units *("U")*.

After a few circuits of light blue beads, the new circuit starts with a red bead. Two light blue beads (*"O"* in the table) are worked

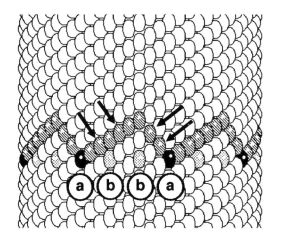

Fig. 9-13. *Any design element starts with a single
bead (a), while the beads
(b) represent the beads
labeled "O" in the table.
For each design-bead on
the "counter-spiral" there is
a mate on the spiral (ar-
rows) when beading this circuit.*

in, then a red one which corresponds to the first unit of the next
design element. After completion of this circuit we will notice that
it contains six red beads. These, multiplied by the units in one
design element, give us 18 units which equals the total number of
units in the circuit (Fig. 9-13).

Just as this mathematical principle underlies the division of the
units and the design elements around the shaft, similar mathematical rules govern the size and shape of each individual design
element: one side of a point or rectangle is always longer than the
other. This interdependence becomes even more intriguing, as the
shorter side of a design element *("S" in the table)*, which falls on
the "counter-spiral" mentioned before, always has one bead more
than the design element has units and its number can be either
even or odd. The long side *("L" in the table)*, however, is always
an odd number and is the sum of the design element units and
the beads of the shorter side (Fig. 9-12). In a continuous band of
design elements, the lowermost bead of a "short side" is also the
first bead of the *next* design element's "long side."

The following formulas should make this calculation easier:

$$S = U+1 \qquad S = L-U$$
$$U = S-1 \qquad U = L-S$$
$$L = 2\,U+1 \qquad L = 2\,S-1 \qquad L = S+U$$
$$O = U-1$$

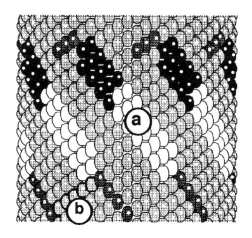

Fig. 9-14. *Isolated slanted design elements such as these feathers look best when they are placed on the counter-spirals.*
(a) Design element.
(b) Imaginary "long" side.

Even the number of circuits necessary to complete the design elements is subject to the principle of triads which controls the *unit-of-three* variant of the gourd-stitch: spirals increase with every circuit; counter-spirals do so with every second circuit; and vertical bead lines have to wait for the third circuit to be continued.

Describing "short" and "long" sides should not imply that only zigzag or parallelogram designs are possible. These terms were rather meant to explain the principles: even a solidly colored area will enable you to project imaginary long or short sides. You can start a "short side" on a counter-spiral which has no "long side" or spiral—an opposite side, existing only in your mind, establishes the starting point for the neighboring design element, such as slanted feather motifs (Fig. 9-14).

This display of mathematical aesthetics in Indian art convinces me that in some way or another most Indian beadworkers have been aware of these principles in their gourd-stitch work, though these may not have been so explicitly defined in formulas. Even while the table was developed to save such reckoning operations, I felt it important to exhibit the interplay of the mathematical elements, inherent to peyote beadwork, at length.

Besides the table and the formula, there is a third way to plan designs and color combinations: graph papers, which you will find in the appendix (pages 196–197). Although these graph papers have been designed to show the round objects in a more-or-less

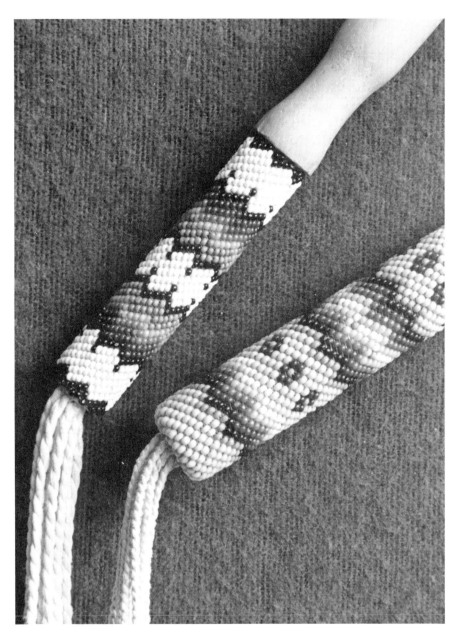

Fig. 9-15. *Two typical examples of gourd-stitch beadwork. Top: The handle of a gourd rattle, beaded by a Quapaw beadworker. Bottom: the handle of a loose-feather fan, collected from the Cheyenne in Oklahoma (Author's Collection).*

three-dimensional way, regard them as another aid only to understand the design principles, rather than making yourself a slave
to strictly outlined designs. Once you have freed yourself from this
device, you will realize that the real enjoyment of this craft is in the
slow build-up of designs while you are working at it. Unlike making
faithful replicas of old-time beadwork with the sewn beading
techniques, gourd-stitch beadwork will always come up with sur-
prising results and experimenting with colors and designs will
never end; each object is a new adventure.

VARIATIONS OF SPIRAL PATTERNS

REVERSING SPIRALS. Spirals can travel either toward the right
or toward the left. Whenever you feel like it, or when the design
suggests doing so, you may reverse the direction of the spiral, and
thus change the pattern's texture. Each uppermost bead of the last
circuit is simply pushed over to the other side (Fig. 9-17). Shifting
the beads will not affect your working direction and you can
continue as before. Each bead shifted will create a tiny gap and

Fig. 9-16. *Close-up of a loose-
feather fan-handle, showing
how spirals change their direction (Beadwork by the author).*

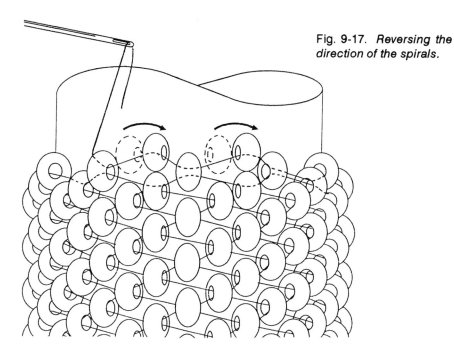

Fig. 9-17. *Reversing the direction of the spirals.*

there's nothing you can do about that. You should not worry, however, about these gaps as human vision is perfectly able to compensate for this and will tend to close the gaps by the surrounding area, particularly in light-colored areas.

Watch out that newly-added beads go on the proper side. During the first circuits after changing the spiral direction, you may have to pay additional attention as the beads often tend to fall into the old position, until a sufficient length of new spirals has been build up.

You will notice that, before reversing the beads, the spirals and the design built up *against* the working direction, while from now on they will go *with* that direction until you reverse the spirals again.

CHEVRON AND DIAMOND PATTERNS.   Although reversing the direction of the spirals was very rarely done by Native beadworkers, these techniques should be included here because they offer some intriguing variations in gourd-stitch patterns. Instead of changing

a   **b**

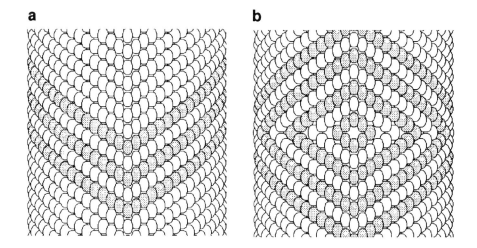

Fig. 9-18. *(a) In chevron patterns, the spirals mirror each other on a vertical line. (b) In diamond patterns, they also mirror on a horizontal line.*

all of the spirals to another direction, you may change only half of them, thus creating a chevron pattern (Fig. 9-19), with spirals diverging symmetrically to the right and left, and meeting again on

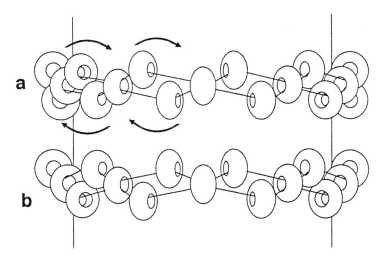

Fig. 9-19. *Starting the chevron pattern. (a) Reversing the slope of the spirals on the left half. (b) Spirals of the left half mirror those of the right half.*

the opposite side. You can do this whenever you have an *even* number of units on both sides of the chevron. As long as this number of units is divisible by two again, it is even possible to add more chevrons in-between which will result in a zigzag pattern of spirals. These meet with their mates at imaginary vertical lines either slanting down in \/-fashion, or slanting up in /\-fashion. The way the beads are worked in at those "meeting-lines" depends on their slant.

Provided you have exchanged the slopes as in Fig. 9-19, you work in beads at the symmetry line of /\-spirals with this sequence, starting with the fourth circuit.

- *4th circuit*: work in two beads, go through the next "uppermost" bead, and continue (Fig. 9-20a).

- *5th circuit*: go through the first of the beads added in the fourth circuit, work in one bead, go through the next bead previously added, and continue (Fig. 9-20b).

- *6th circuit*: go through the bead added in the fifth circuit, without working in a bead, through the next "uppermost" bead and continue (Fig. 9-20c).

For \/-spirals the sequence is different.

- *4th circuit*: go through the next "uppermost" bead, without working in a new bead, and continue (Fig. 9-20d).

- *5th circuit*: work in one bead, go through the next "uppermost" bead, and continue (Fig. 9-20e).

- *6th circuit*: work in one bead, go through the bead added in the fifth circuit, work in another bead, go through the next "uppermost" bead, and continue (Fig. 9-20f).

In both cases, the seventh circuit starts these cycles again. While adding new beads comes to you almost automatically, you have to pay special attention when the chevron's spirals merge.

Although *diamond* patterns may look still more difficult, they are simply a reversal of chevron patterns (Fig. 9-18b), and the same method as described for reversing spirals applies here. Of course, you have to observe constantly the correct sequence of working in the beads, and I would recommend that you master the

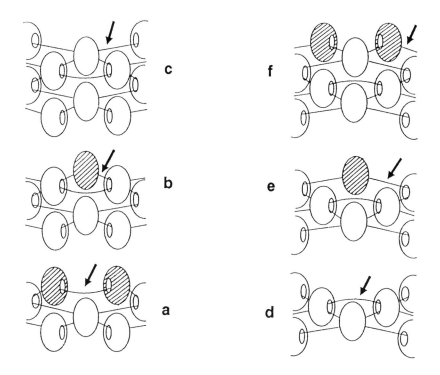

Fig. 9-20. *As spirals meet each other in chevron patterns, a special sequence must be observed when working in new beads (shown from* bottom *to* top*). (a–c) For /\-spirals. (d–f) For \/-spirals. Arrows indicate the thread of the current circuit.*

basic techniques of the gourd-stitch before you embark on ambitious projects with diamond patterns.

DESIGNS IN CHEVRON AND DIAMOND PATTERNS. In the basic pattern which does not interrupt the course of the spirals, you usually work with bands of zigzags or parallelograms, or isolated designs on the counter-spirals. Chevron and diamond patterns, on the other hand, with their symmetries, offer ample use for designs with lines not prescribed by the pattern (Fig. 9-21c & d). While they do not blend very well with the basic pattern as I have found out,

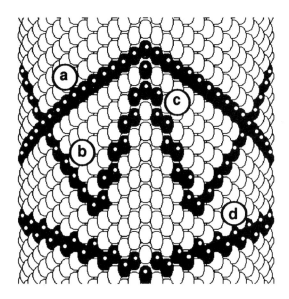

Fig. 9-21. *Chevron patterns permit design lines at angles not easily used in the basic pattern. (a) and (b) are the lines commonly used on spirals and counterspirals. Lines such as (c) and (d) make any kind of designs possible, as the symmetry line keeps them in balance.*

they work perfectly with the chevron or diamond pattern, as they mirror with their counterparts, and may or may not meet at the symmetry lines. Together with the regular spirals and counter-spirals and a tasteful and imaginative use of colors, you will encounter an endless array of design variations, and placing the emphasis of the design elements on the "counterspirals" will greatly enhance your gourd-stitch beadwork.

ADDING NEW UNITS

While ceremonial staffs, rattles, tail-dance sticks, and most loose-feather fan-handles maintain their width or diameter throughout their lengths, *flat fan-handles* have a tapering shape and usually feature a fixed set of tail feathers of golden eagles, hawks, or waterbirds. Because of the increasing circumference, this tapering confronts the beadworker with new problems: if you tried to continue using the same number of beads, you will soon end up with gaps becoming larger and larger. To overcome this problem you have to use a different approach.

Fig. 9-22. *Set of peyote instruments, beaded by Burnett Iron Shell (Museum für Völkerkunde, Berlin, Germany; photograph by Friedrich Graf).*

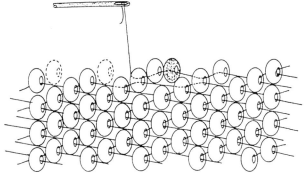

Fig. 9-23. *To expand gourd-stitch beadwork, you have to add new units or spirals. Working in two beads at the same time in the first circuit of expanding starts the new spiral.*

- First circuit: *two* beads instead of one are picked up at the same time wherever a new unit has to be added. Seen from the needle's eye, the second bead marks the beginning of the new spiral or unit (Fig. 9-23).

- In the second circuit, one bead is added which will be the second bead of the new spiral, with passing the thread through the first bead of the new spiral. Pull back the thread to make room for the next new bead. After going through the next bead, add new beads until this circuit is completed (Fig. 9-24).

- To bead the third circuit, add a new bead, go with the thread through the second bead of the new spiral, work in another bead, and after passing through the next bead, continue in the regular gourd-stitch fashion (Fig. 9-25d).

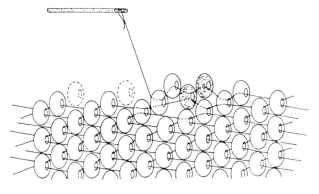

Fig. 9-24. *In the second circuit of expanding, the new beads are worked next to those of the previous circuit.*

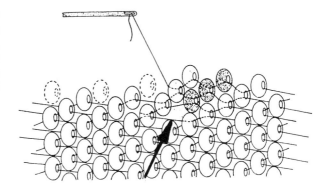

Fig. 9-25. *Beading the third circuit when adding a new spiral. (Arrow points to gap resulting from starting a new spiral.)*

The tiny gap thus created cannot be avoided and becomes less noticeable, depending on the size of the beads. You will be able to proceed for a few circuits before you feel the need for adding more units.

Though technically very easy to accomplish, expanding or adding new units in the basic pattern, with spirals winding around the shaft until your beadwork is completed, requires careful planning. Your design combinations permitting, you should try to add new units in the solidly-colored background area. Don't start your fan handle with a fixed plan of designs; instead, adjust development of designs to the units added. When and where new units should be added depends to a great deal on the shape and size of your object as well as the degree of its taper. As in the beginning of your work, take care that the total number of units in a circuit will not result in a prime number, otherwise design elements will not divide evenly. I also would suggest to start adding units when *two* new units are needed in order to assure a smooth progression of the designs.

Adding units in chevron patterns is much easier, as the spirals meet at their symmetry line(s). Remember how beads are worked in on these symmetry lines (Fig. 9-20); all you have do is to work in *two* beads where you have inserted one bead in the regular chevron pattern. On fan handles with only a slight taper, you may have to work in two beads at a few of those circuits before adding another *single* bead in-between, while on handles with a circumfer-

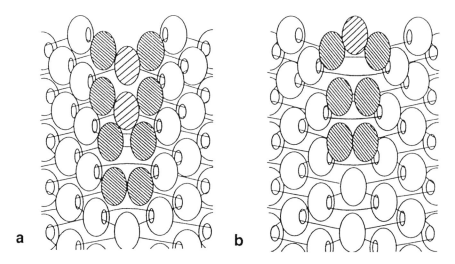

Fig. 9-26. *Adding units in chevron patterns. Different hatching shows which of the new beads belongs to which circuit. (a) In spirals meeting at a downward slant. (b) In spirals meeting at an upward slant.*

ence expanding more rapidly, you might alternate adding two beads in one circuit with one bead in the next appropriate circuit (Fig. 9-26).

"UNIT-OF-TWO" PATTERN

Most "how-to" books on Indian beadwork leave the impression that another, simpler form of the gourd-stitch is the only netting technique available: here the units are made up of two beads only. Consistent with the "unit-of-three pattern," it could be aptly called the "*unit-of-two* pattern." Surprisingly, this variant of the gourd-stitch has never been very popular among Native beadworkers: except for colors and designs, its pattern is less sophisticated and does not allow for variations. It has been my own experience that the unit-of-two pattern is more difficult to start with when you work with very small beads—in the unit-of-three method the spirals form immediately the typical pattern and the beads fall very easily into their place; it takes much longer to complete one circuit, and unless

Fig. 9-27. *Though apparently popular among non-Indian beadworkers, the unit-of-two pattern has much more limited variations in patterns and designs.*

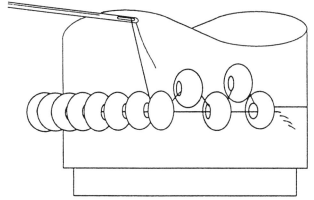

the beads are perfectly uniform, it will not be easy to achieve real straight vertical bead lines.

Recall that, in the unit-of-three method, the number of beads to start with should be divisible by three, with one-third removed at the beginning. In the unit-of-two gourd-stitching, however, the total number for the circumference must be divisible by *two*, and *half* of these beads must be removed. To achieve enough tension on the thread, it should be wrapped twice around the shaft before running the needle through the first bead of the first circuit and tightening it by pulling it back. Pick up a bead, and, instead of skipping the next bead, pass the thread through this *first* one. Another bead is picked up and the needle drawn through the bead next in line, and so on (Fig. 9-27). Stepping up to the next is done the same way we have learned with the unit-of-three variation.

Designs and design elements orient themselves as vertical bead lines and diagonals running symmetrically toward both left and right. You will have noticed that in unit-of-three beading a perfect lateral symmetry cannot be established; there the slightly off-balanced design elements are a characteristic trait.

COMANCHE-STITCH

When you rotate a "unit-of-two"-beaded object by 90° you will notice that the same pattern takes a totally different look: now the beads align horizontally opposing the vertical alignment we have dealt with hitherto. The new pattern reminds us of a brick wall, accounting for the term *brick-stitch*, another popular name for the Comanche-stitch which makes use of the new layout. Designs now form in a horizontal fashion with diagonals running in both directions. Here, however, the similarities of "unit-of-two" gourd-stitch and Comanche-stitch end. Two major traits govern the Comanche-stitch: beads no longer act as "knots;" these are rather placed in between; the technique's individual steps differ completely from the previous variations, and relate more to *single-bead edging*.

Fig. 9-28. *Close-up of Comanche-stitch.*

Fig. 9-29. *Beading
the first circuit in the
Comanche-stitch.
Each circuit starts
with* two *beads.*

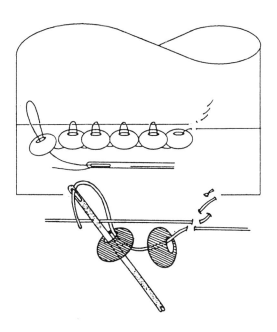

BEADING THE FIRST CIRCUIT. The thread is backstitched into the leather, wrapped once around the shaft, and, next to the first backstitches, fastened again; this starting wrap is commonly called the *base-thread* (Fig. 9-29). Pick up *two* beads, and, from below, pass the needle *under* the base-thread thread and return it through the *second* bead, or the bead next to the needle's tip; pull through the full length of the thread and tighten it with the usual backward pull. Now pick up only one bead at a time, but proceed in the same fashion, always pulling the thread under the base-thread and back through the bead. As a result, the beads of this first circuit will lean around the shaft, exposing their holes. Do not worry about this because this is quite natural: the second circuit will force the beads to assume their correct position. In the Comanche-stitch, each circuit also represents a "row" which is the only structural element of the pattern. But to be consistent and avoid confusion I prefer to continue using the term "circuit."

BEADING THE SECOND CIRCUIT. Having completed the first circuit, pass the needle through the first bead of the first circuit.

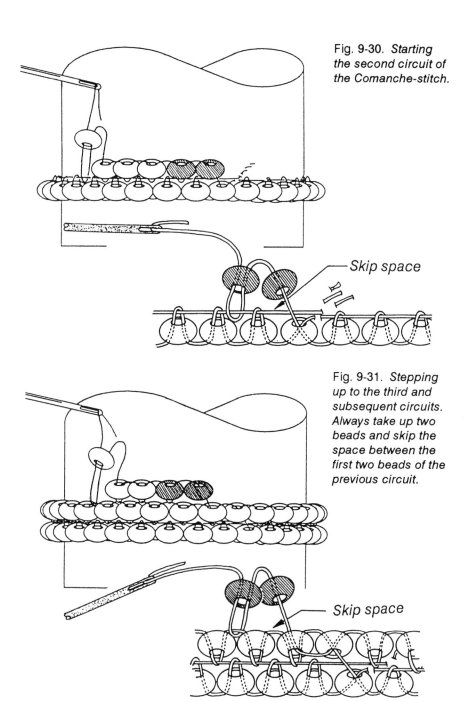

Fig. 9-30. *Starting the second circuit of the Comanche-stitch.*

Skip space

Fig. 9-31. *Stepping up to the third and subsequent circuits. Always take up two beads and skip the space between the first two beads of the previous circuit.*

Skip space

Again, pick up *two* beads, and, skipping the space between the first and the second bead of the first circuit, pass the thread *behind* the base-thread and return through the bead, remembering to tighten the thread. As the beads of the first circuit lean quite tightly against the shaft, getting the needle behind the base thread and between the beads might be the most difficult part of the Comanche-stitch; it will take some patience to work in the beads for the second circuit. As in the first circuit, continue using *one* bead at a time only (Fig. 9-30).

BEADING THE THIRD CIRCUIT. After having worked in the last bead of the second circuit, pass the needle from *above* through the *first* bead of the second circuit and from *below* through the bead next to it—do not forget to tug the thread. As before, two beads are picked up to start the third circuit, and skipping the space (or loop) neighboring the emerging thread the needle is pulled through the next loop (Fig. 9-31). To complete this circuit, work as usually in the one-bead-at-a-time rhythm. Remember to begin each new circuit in the same fashion, as taking up two beads

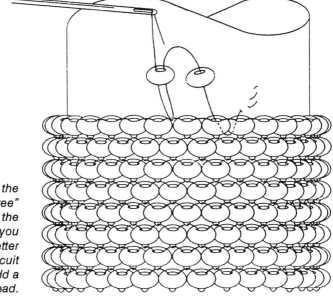

Fig. 9-32. *As in the "unit-of-three" pattern, in the Comanche-stitch you should better complete a circuit before you add a new thread.*

and skipping the first loop creates the staggered alignment of the beads which characterizes the Comanche-stitch.

ADDING NEW THREAD.   Whenever you have to start a new thread, do this after you have completed a circuit. With a couple of backstitches sew down the end of the old thread and cut it off. Add the new thread with a few backstitches—this can be done at any place as long as you fasten the new thread very close to the last circuit. From above, pass the needle through the nearest bead and back through the adjacent bead (Fig. 9-32). Pull the thread taut, take up two beads to start the new circuit, and continue working as usual.

Going into each detail and variation of the gourd-stitch or Comanche-stitch would call for a gourd-stitch book of its own! Though pretty much attracted by peyote beadwork, I would not regard myself as an expert, and I see little sense in "re-inventing the wheel" by competing with Richard Past's well-researched instructions on the manifold variations of the gourd-stitch. I simply have tried to offer a different approach to these beading techniques and strongly recommend that you to study his writing carefully.

APPENDIX

HOW TO USE THE BEAD GRAPH PAPERS

Although most advanced beadworkers will question the usefulness of such graph papers, I have included them for the novice bead-worker. For your personal use, you may photocopy them, but once you feel familiar with the various beading techniques, you should try to free yourself from these "crutches" and approach Indian style beadwork as the Native beadworkers did.

To use the graph paper on page 194 for lane-stitch beadwork, decide on the number of beads that should go on a *bead row*, and with ruler and pencil draw lines which will stand for the *lanes* you want to bead. Although theoretically possible, I would not recommend using this graph paper for geometric overlay-stitch bead-work. Unless you use perfectly even-sized beads your beadwork will never be as exact as the design(s) on the graph paper. Neatness of overlay-stitch beading as well as alignment of the designs are judged by the eye and, as stated before, slight irregularities will add some touch to your beadwork.

The graph paper for loomwork (page 195) is probably self-ex-planatory and can be used for any kind of woven beadwork. Consult pages 150–152 on how to use this type of graph paper for diagonal weaving.

The graph papers for gourd-stitch and Comanche-stitch bead-work have been designed to show how the designs actually will look on a three-dimensional object, such as a fan handle.

Graph Paper for Lane-Stitch

Graph Paper for Woven Beadwork

Graph Paper for Gourd-Stitch Designs

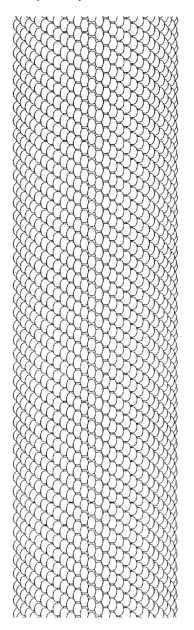

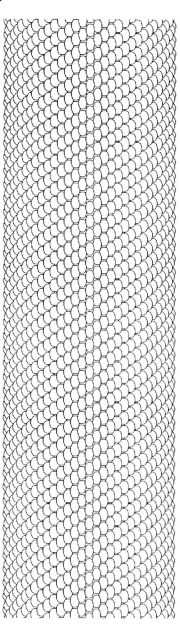

Spirals ascending to the left   *Spirals ascending to the right*

Graph Paper for Gourd-Stitch Designs

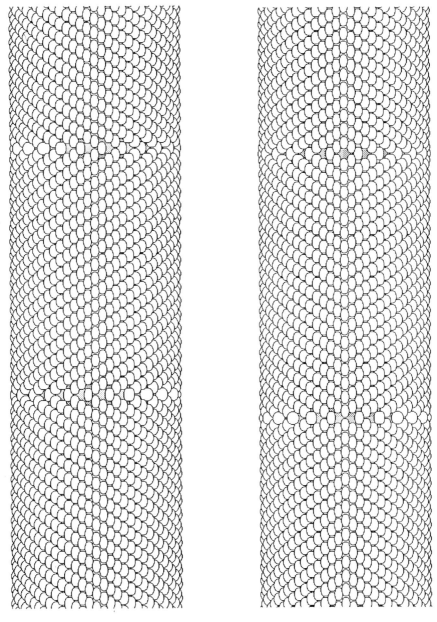

Reversing Spirals

Chevron & Diamond Pattern

Graph Paper for Gourd-Stitch Designs

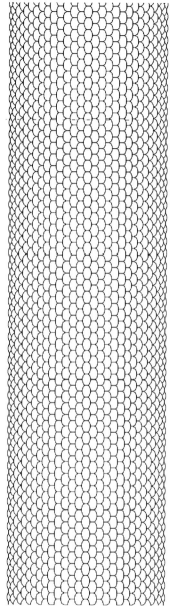

"Unit-of-Two" Pattern

Comanche-Stitch

BIBLIOGRAPHY

A. HISTORY OF BEADS

ANONYMOUS:
  1971 "The Enduring Intrigue of Glass Trade Beads." *Arizona Highways*, Vol. 47, No. 7: 10–37.
CONN, Richard G.:
  1972 "The Pony Bead Period: a Cultural Problem of Western North America." *Society for Historical Archaeology Newsletter*, Vol. 5: 7–13.
DUBIN, Lois S.:
  1987 *The History of Beads: From 30.000 B.C. to the Present.* New York: Abrams.
FRANCIS, Peter Jr.:
  1979a *The Story of Venetian Beads.* Lake Placid, New York: Lapis Route Books. (The World of Beads Monograph Series. Vol. 1.)
  1979b *The Czech Bead Story.* Lake Placid, New York: Lapis Route Books. (The World of Beads Monograph Series. Vol. 2.)

B. BEADING TECHNIQUES

BUGELSKI, Peter:
  1989 "Lazy Stitch Beadwork." *Whispering Wind: Crafts Annual.* No. 2:34–42. [Reprint of an article published in 1977]
CHANDLER, Milford G. & David A. KRACINSKI:
  1962 "Unusual Beadwork Techniques, Pt. 1: A Classification System and a Study of Cross Weaving." *American Indian Tradition*, Vol. 8, No. 5: 197–206.
  1963 "Unusual Beadwork Techniques, Pt. 2: Strip Netting." *American Indian Tradition*, Vol. 9, No. 1: 38–40.
CONN, Richard G.:
  1960 "Beadwork with Style." *American Indian Hobbyist*, Vol. 6, Nos. 7 & 8: 79–85.
FEDER, Norman:
  1961 "An Unusual Beadwork Technique." *American Indian Tradition*, Vol. 8, No. 1: 41–42.

HOLM, Bill:
  1985   "Old Photos Might Not Lie, But They Fib a Lot about Color!"
  American Indian Art Magazine, Vol. 10, No. 4: 44–49.
LESSARD, F. Dennis:
  1968   "The Kickapoo Stitch." *Powwow Trails*. Vol. 5, No. 5: 56– 57.
LOTTER, John:
  1973   "Heddle Loom Beading." *American Indian Crafts and Culture*,
  Vol. 7, No. 7: 2–7.
MILLER, Preston:
  1971   *Four Winds Indian Beadwork & Old Flathead Photos. A Manual
  of Beading Techniques*. St. Ignatius, Montana.
MOSS, Kathlyn & Alice SCHERER:
  1992   *The New Beadwork.* New York: Abrams.
ORCHARD, William C.:
  1929   *Beads and Beadwork of the American Indians*. New York: Museum of the American Indian, Heye Foundation. (Contributions
  from the Museum of the American Indian, Heye Foundation. Vol.
  11.)
PAST, Richard E.:
  1969a "American Indian Net Beadwork, Pt 1: The Basic Technique."
  Powwow Trails, Vol. 6, No. 1: 11–16.
  1969b "American Indian Net Beadwork, Pt 2: Unit Addition." *Powwow
  Trails*, Vol. 6, No. 2: 34–36.
  1969c "American Indian Net Beadwork, Pt 3: Variations." *Powwow
  Trails*, Vol. 6, No. 5: 85–91.
  1990   "Gourd Stitch: A Complete Study of Techniques and Designs
  of the Basic Stitch, Expansion, Comanche Style, and Chevron
  Patterns". *Whispering Wind: Crafts Annual*. No. 3:4–37. [Reprint
  of a series of articles published in 1985]
SCHNEIDER, Richard C.:
  1972   *Crafts of the North American Indians: a Craftsman's Manual*.
  Stevens Point, Wisconsin: Schneider Publ.
STEWART, Tyrone H.:
  1969a "Peyote Beadwork Technique, Pt. 1." *American Indian Crafts
  and Culture*, Vol. 3, No. 1: 2–10.
  1969b "Peyote Beadwork Technique, Pt. 2." *American Indian Crafts
  and Culture*, Vol. 3, No. 9: 1.
STONE, Ben:
  1971   "Applique Beadwork." *American Indian Crafts and Culture*, Vol.
  5, No. 1: 2–5.

C. PLAINS IN GENERAL

FEDER, Norman:
  1987　"Bird Quillwork." *American Indian Art Magazine*, Vol. 12, No. 3: 46–57.
GALLAGHER, Orvoell R. & Louis H. POWELL:
  1953　"Time Perspective in Plains Indian Beaded Art." *American Anthropologist*, N. S., 55: 608–613.
HOLM, Bill:
  1958　"Plains Indian Cloth Dresses." *American Indian Hobbyist*, Vol. 4, No. 5 & 6: 43–47.
LAMB, Gerald:
  1983　*Authentication and Dating of Plains Art*. Santa Fe: Canfield.
LESSARD, F. Dennis:
  1980　"Problems Related to Tribal Identification of Plains Indian Art." *Plains Indian Design Symbology and Decoration*. Cody, Wyoming: Buffalo Bill Historical Center: 31–38.
POHRT, Richard A.:
  1977　"Plains Indian Moccasins with Decorated Soles." *American Indian Art Magazine*, Vol. 2, No. 3: 32–39, 84.
SCHNEIDER, Mary Jane:
  1980　"Plains Indian Art." *Anthropology on the Great Plains*. Ed. by W. R. Wood & M. Liberty. Lincoln, Nebraska: University of Nebraska Press: 197–211.
  1983　"The Production of Indian-Use and Souvenir Beadwork by Contemporary Indian Women." *Plains Anthropologist*, Vol. 28, No. 102: 235–245.

D. CENTRAL PLAINS

BREWER, Robert:
  1976　"A Beaded Purse." *Indian America*, Vol. 9, No. 2: 56–57.
CHRONISTER, Allen:
  1990　"Arapaho Beadwork." *Whispering Wind*, Vol. 23, No. 6: 4–9.
COLEMAN, Winfield W.:
  1980　"The Cheyenne Women's Sewing Society." *Plains Indian Design Symbology and Decoration*. Cody, Wyoming: Buffalo Bill Historical Center: 50–69.
CONN, Richard G.:
  1960　"Western Sioux Beadwork." *American Indian Hobbyist*, Vol. 6, Nos. 9 & 10: 113–123.

1961 "Cheyenne Style Beadwork." *American Indian Hobbyist*, Vol. 7, No. 2: 47–62.

GREEN, Richard:
1990 "Cheyenne Cradle Covers." *Whispering Wind*, Vol. 23, No. 3: 4–12.

HAIL, Barbara A.:
1988 "Beaded Bibles and Victory Pouches: 20th Century Lakota Honoring Gifts." *American Indian Art Magazine*, Vol. 13, No. 3: 40–47.

HABERLAND, Wolfgang:
1986 *Ich, Dakota: Pine Ridge Reservation 1909.* Berlin: Reimer.

JOHNSON, Michael G.:
1967 "Cheyenne Pipe Bag." *Powwow Trails*, Vol. 4, No. 1: 6.
1968 "19th Century Cheyenne Moccasins." *Powwow Trails*, Vol. 4, No. 10: 4–6.
1969a "Western Sioux Man's Costume 1880-1910, Pt. 1." *Powwow Trails*, Vol. 6, No. 1: 4–8.
1969b "Western Sioux Man's Costume 1880-1910, Pt. 2." *Powwow Trails*, Vol. 6, No. 2: 25–29.
1969c "Western Sioux Man's Costume 1880-1910, Pt. 3." *Powwow Trails*, Vol. 6, No. 3: 45–51.

KOSTELNIK, Michael J.:
1985 "Classic Cheyenne Moccasins." *Moccasin Tracks*, Vol. 11, No. 4: 4–5.

LANFORD, Benson L.:
1990a "Origins of Central Plains Beadwork." *American Indian Art Magazine*, Vol. 16, No. 1: 72–79.
1990b "Belt Pouches in the Derby Collection." *Eye of the Angel.* Ed. by David Wooley. Northampton, Massachusetts: White Star Press: 56–60.

LESSARD, F. Dennis:
1984 "Instruments of Prayer: the Peyote Art of the Sioux." *American Indian Art Magazine*, Vol. 9, No. 2: 24–27.
1990a "Defining the Central Plains Art Area." *American Indian Art Magazine*, Vol. 16, No. 1: 36–43.
1990b "Pictographic Art in Beadwork from the Cheyenne River Sioux." *American Indian Art Magazine*, Vol. 16, No. 1: 54–63.
1991 "Pictographic Sioux Beadwork: a Re-Examination." *American Indian Art Magazine*, Vol. 16, No. 4: 70–74.

LESSARD, Rosemary T.:
  1980   "A Short Historical Survey of Lakota Women's Clothing." *Plains Indian Design Symbology and Decoration*. Cody: Buffalo Bill Historical Center: 70–76.
  1990   "Lakota Cradles." *American Indian Art Magazine*, Vol. 16, No. 1: 44–53.
LYFORD, Carrie:
  1983   *Quill and Beadwork of the Western Sioux*. [Reprint of the 1940 edition.] Stevens Point, Wisconsin: Schneider Publ.
NIMERFRO, Steve:
  1982   "Sioux Style Lazy Stitch Beadwork." *Moccasin Tracks*, Vol. 7, No. 7: 6–7.
POWERS, Marla:
  1986   *Oglala Women: Myth, Ritual and Reality*. Chicago: University of Chicago Press.
STEWART, Tyrone H.:
  1971a "Cheyenne Moccasins, Pt. 1." *American Indian Crafts and Culture*, Vol. 5, No. 8: 2–8, 14–17.
  1971b "Cheyenne Moccasins, Pt. 2." *American Indian Crafts and Culture*, Vol. 5, No. 9: 2–8,18.
TUCKER, Michael S.:
  1969   *Old Time Sioux Dancers*. Tulsa, Oklahoma: American Indian Crafts and Culture.

E.   NORTHERN PLAINS

BATES, Craig D.:
  1983   "A Cree Pipebag." *Moccasin Tracks*, Vol. 8, No. 6: 12–13.
BRASSER, Ted J.:
  1984   "Backrest Banners Among the Plains Cree and Plains Ojibwa." *American Indian Art Magazine*, Vol. 10, No. 1: 56–63.
CONN, Richard G.:
  1958   "Costumes of the Northern Plains." *American Indian Hobbyist*, Vol. 5, Nos. 1 & 2: 2–20.
  1961   "Blackfeet Women's Clothing." *American Indian Hobbyist*, Vol. 7, No. 4: 113–127.
  1989   "Blackfeet Women's Clothing: A Complete Study of Blackfeet Women's Clothing from Pre-1815 to Present." *Whispering Wind: Crafts Annual*. No. 2:5–31. [Reprint of an article published in 1984]

1990   "Blackfoot Clothing Style." *The Scriver Blackfoot Collection: Repatriation of Canada's Heritage*. Ed. by Philip H. R. Stepney & David J. Goa. Edmonton Canada: Provincial Museum of Alberta: 79–101.

DINGMAN, Sid:
1971   "Woman's Northern Dress." *Whispering Wind*, Vol. 5, No. 7: 105–111.

EWERS, John C.:
1986   *Blackfeet Crafts*. [Reprint of the 1945 edition.] Stevens Point, Wisconsin: Schneider Publ.

FEDER, Norman:
1968   "Blackfeet War Shirt." *Singing Wire*, Vol. 2, No. 4: 6.

HUNGRY WOLF, Adolf & Beverly:
1977   *Blackfoot Craftworker's Book*. Invermere, B.C. (Good Medicine No. 15.)

JOHNSON, Michael G.:
1966   "Blackfeet Costume 1910-1960." *Powwow Trails*, Vol. 3, Nos. 5–6: 6–17.
1969   "Indian Beadwork from the Canadian Plains." *Powwow Trails*, Vol. 5, No. 6: 119–121.
1971   "Early Northern Plains Shirt and Legging: Examples from British Collections." *American Indian Crafts and Culture*, Vol. 5, No. 10: 2–7.
1971   "Late Blackfeet Shirts and Leggings." *American Indian Crafts and Culture*, Vol. 5, No. 6: 3–7.

POHRT, Richard A.:
1989   "Tribal Identification of Northern Plains Beadwork." *American Indian Art Magazine*, Vol. 15, No. 1: 72–79.

SCRIVER, Bob:
1990   *The Blackfeet: Artists of the Northern Plains; The Scriver Collection of Blackfeet Indian Artifacts and Related Objects, 1894–1990*. Kansas City, Missouri: Lowell Press.

WARNER, John Anson:
1990   "Continuity & Change in Modern Plains Cree Moccasins." *American Indian Art Magazine*, Vol. 15, No. 3: 36–47.

WEST, Ian & Michael G. JOHNSON:
1966a   "Northern Plains Gun Cases, pt 1." *Powwow Trails*, Vol. 2, No. 8: 3–7.
1966b   "Northern Plains Gun Cases, pt 2." *Powwow Trails*, Vol. 2, No. 9: 3–5.

F. TRANSMONTANE STYLE (CROW & PLATEAU)

BREWER, Robert:
1983 "Crow Blanket Strips & Crow Stitch." *Moccasin Tracks*, Vol. 8, No. 7: 10–11.
1987 "A Pair of Crow Moccasins." *Moccasin Tracks*, Vol. 12, No. 1: 9–11.

COFFEY, Larry:
1959 "Crow Shirt." *American Indian Hobbyist*, Vol. 5, No. 7,8: 81–83.

DOUGLAS, Frederic H.:
1937 *A Crow Beaded Horse Collar*. Denver: Denver Art Museum: 5–9. (Material Culture Notes 2).

DUNCAN, Kate:
1991 "Beadwork on the Plateau." *A Time of Gathering: Native Heritage in Washington State*. Robin K. Wright, ed. Seattle: Burke Museum & University of Washington Press: 189–196.

DYCK, Paul:
1988 "Elegance Mingled with Beauty." *To Honor the Crow People: Crow Indian Art from the Goelet and Edith Gallatin Collection of American Indian Art*. Ed. by Peter J. Powell & Ann S. Merritt. Chicago: Foundation for the Preservation of American Indian Art and Culture, Inc.: 9–11.

FEDER, Norman:
1980a "Crow Blanket Strip Rosettes." *American Indian Art Magazine*, Vol. 6, No. 1: 40–45.
1980b "Crow Indian Art—the Problem." *American Indian Art Magazine*, Vol. 6, No. 1: 30–31.

GALANTE, Gary:
1980 "Crow Lance Cases or Sword Scabbards." *American Indian Art Magazine*, Vol. 6, No. 1: 64–73.
1984 "East Meets West: Some Observations on the Crow as the Nexus of Plateau/Upper Missouri River Art." *Crow Indian Art Symposium paper*. Mission, South Dakota: Chandler Institute: 49–60.

HOLM, Bill:
1981 "Crow-Nez Perce Otterskin Bowcase-Quivers." *American Indian Art Magazine*, Vol. 6, No. 4: 60–70.
1984 "Crow-Plateau Beadword: an Effort toward a Uniform Terminology." *Crow Indian Art Symposium paper*. Mission, South Dakota: Chandler Institute: 27–32.

JOHNSON, Michael R.:
1959 "Crow Leggings." *American Indian Hobbyist*, Vol. 5, No. 5–6: 65–66.
JOHNSTON, James:
1969 "Contemporary Crow Costuming." *Powwow Trails*, Vol. 6, No. 6: 105–112.
JULL, Louie:
1959 "Crow-Type Shirt Strips." *American Indian Hobbyist*, Vol. 5, No. 5–6: 57–58.
LANFORD, Benson L.:
1980 "Parfleche and Crow Beadwork Designs." *American Indian Art Magazine*, Vol. 6, No. 1: 32–39.
1984 "Beadwork and Parfleche Designs." *Crow Indian Art Symposium Paper.* Mission, South Dakota: Chandler Institute: 7–14.
LESSARD, F. Dennis:
1980 "Crow Indian Art—the Nez Perce Connection." *American Indian Art Magazine*, Vol. 6, No. 1: 54–63.
1984 "Classic Crow Beadwork: Upper Missouri River Roots." *Crow Indian Art Symposium Paper.* Mission, South Dakota: Chandler Institute: 61–68.
LOEB, Barbara:
1979 *An Analysis of Crow Beadwork: Why Won't the Light Blue Stay in the Background.* Paper Read at New Directions in Native American Art, University of New Mexico, Albuquerque.
1980 "Mirror Bags and Bandoleer Bags, a Comparison." *American Indian Art Magazine*, Vol. 6, No. 1: 46–53, 88.
1983 *Classic Intermontane Beadwork: Art of the Crow and Plateau Tribes.* Ph.D. Dissertation. Seattle: University of Washington.
1984a "An Update on Crow Beadwork: Authors, Beadwork, and Living Crow Artists." *Fifth Annual Plains Indian Seminar in Honor of Dr. John C. Ewers.* Ed. by George P. Horse Capture and Gene Ball. Cody, Wyoming: Buffalo Bill Historical Center: 133–143.
1984b "Crow and Plateau Beadwork in Black and White: a Study Using Old Photographs." *Crow Indian Art Symposium Paper.* Mission, South Dakota: Chandler Institute: 15–26.
1991 "Dress Me in Color: Transmontane Beading." *A Time of Gathering: Native Heritage in Washington State.* Robin K. Wright, ed. Seattle: Burke Museum & University of Washington Press: 197–201.
LOWIE, Robert H.:
1922 "Crow Indian Art." *Anthropological Papers / American Museum of Natural History.* 21,4: 271–322.

MERRITT, Ann S.:
   1988   "Women's Beaded Robes: Artistic Reflections of the Crow
         World." *To Honor the Crow People: Crow Indian Art from the
         Goelet and Edith Gallatin collection of American Indian Art.* Ed.
         by Peter J. Powell & Ann S. Merritt. Chicago: Foundation for the
         Preservation of American Indian Art and Culture, Inc.: 41–47.
MILLER, Mike & Scott THOMPSON:
   1979   "Spokane Beadwork." *Whispering Wind*, Vol. 12, No. 4: 4–9, 11.
O'CONNOR, Nancy F.:
   1985   *Fred E. Miller: Photographer of the Crows.* Exhibition catalog.
         Missoula: University of Montana; Malibu, California: Carnan
         VidFilm.
POHRT, Richard Jr.:
   1984   "Crow Agency: the Fred Miller Photographs." *Crow Indian Art
         Symposium paper.* Mission, South Dakota: Chandler Institute:
         1–6.
WARD, John:
   1970   "Modern Crow Men's Dance Outfit; pt 2: Beadwork." *American
         Indian Crafts and Culture.* Vol. 4, No. 4: 3–6.
WILDSCHUT, William & John C. EWERS:
   1959   *Crow Indian Beadwork. A Descriptive and Historical Study.* New
         York: Museum of the American Indian. (Contributions from the
         Museum of the American Indian, Heye Foundation. Vol. 16.)

G. SOUTHERN PLAINS

CONN, Richard G.:
   1976   "Southern Plains Beadwork in the Fred Harvey Fine Arts Collec-
         tion." *Fred Harvey Fine Arts Collection.* An exhibition organized
         by the Heard Museum. Phoenix, Arizona: Heard Museum.
COOLEY, Jim:
   1983   "Kiowa Tab Leggings: a Most Elaborate Pair." *Moccasin Tracks*,
         Vol. 8, No. 10: 8–11.
   1984   "Beaded Bolos Oklahoma Style." *Moccasin Tracks*, Vol. 9, No.
         7: 10–14.
   1986a "Southern Plains Women's Footwear, Pt. 1: Examples from 3
         Private Collections." *Moccasin Tracks*, Vol. 11, No. 5: 4–13.
   1986b "Southern Plains Women's Footwear, Pt. 2: Cheyenne Moc-
         casins and the Mohonk Lodge." *Moccasin Tracks*, Vol. 11, No.
         6: 4–13.

DOUGLAS, Frederic H.:
  1937   *A Cheyenne Peyote Fan*. Denver: Denver Art Museum. (Material
         Culture Notes 12).
HAYS, Joe S.:
  1985   "A Skin Shirt, Leggings and their Beaded Borders." *Moccasin
         Tracks*, Vol. 10, No. 8: 10–12.
  1985   "Comanche Tab Leggings." *Moccasin Tracks*, Vol. 11, No. 1:
         4–12.
RIDSON, Tom, Jerry SMITH & Kaysee TSUJI:
  1983   "An Eagle Tail Peyote Fan." *Moccasin Tracks*, Vol. 9, No. 4: 8–9.
  1984a "A Waterbird Fan." *Moccasin Tracks*, Vol. 9, No. 5: 10–13.
  1984b "A Second Eagle Tail Fan." *Moccasin Tracks*, Vol. 9, No. 6:
         10–12.
  1984c "Third Eagle Tail Fan." *Moccasin Tracks*, Vol. 9, No. 10: 4–6.
  1984d "Two Flat Fans." *Moccasin Tracks*, Vol. 10, No. 3: 4–7.
  1984e "Three Flat Fans." *Moccasin Tracks*, Vol. 10, No. 4: 7–9.
  1985   "A Classic Loose Fan." *Moccasin Tracks*, Vol. 10, No. 5: 8–9.
SCHNEIDER, Mary Jane:
  1983   "Kiowa and Comanche Baby Carriers." *Plains Anthropologist*,
         Vol. 28, No. 102: 305–314.
SMITH, Jerry:
  1981   "Southern Plains Leggings: Red Rolled Fringe." *Moccasin
         Tracks*, Vol. 6, No. 10: 10–11.
  1983a "A Pair of Kiowa Tab Leggings." *Moccasin Tracks*, Vol. 8, No. 6:
         6–9.
  1983b "Kiowa Tab Leggings, a Second Pair." *Moccasin Tracks*, Vol. 8,
         No. 7: 8–9.
  1983c "More Kiowa High-Top Moccasins." *Moccasin Tracks*, Vol. 9,
         No. 4: 7.
  1984   "Fan Creations." *Moccasin Tracks*, Vol. 10, No. 2: 4–6.
TSUJI, Kaysee:
  1981   "Fans from the Gilcrease Collection." *Moccasin Tracks*, Vol. 7,
         No. 2: 4–8.
WIEDMAN, Dennis:
  1985   "Staff, Fan, Rattle & Drum: Spiritual and Artistic Expressions of
         Oklahoma Peyotists." *American Indian Art Magazine*, Vol. 10,
         No. 3: 39–45.
WOOLEY, David:
  1990   "Kiowa Belt Pouches in the Derby Collection." *Eye of the Angel*.
         Ed. by David Wooley. Northampton, Massachusetts: White Star
         Press: 51–56.

H. WOODLANDS, GREAT LAKES, METIS, SUBARCTIC AND FLORAL STYLE

ANDERSON, Marcia & Kathy HUSSEY-ARNTSON:
  1986 "Ojibwe Bandolier Bags in the Collection of the Minnesota Historical Society." *American Indian Art Magazine*, Vol. 11, No. 4: 46–57.
BRASSER, Ted J.:
  1990 "Firebags of the Fur Trade." *Eye of the Angel*. Ed. by David Wooley. Northampton, Massachusetts: White Star Press: 35–39.
COOLEY, Jim:
  1985 "The Abstract Floral Clout: a Study in Material Culture Diffusion." *Moccasin Tracks*, Vol. 10, No. 9: 4–13.
DEHANADISONKWE:
  1973 "Native Dress and Design among the Iroquoian People." *American Indian Crafts and Culture*, Vol. 7, No. 5: 5–9,15.
DUNCAN, Kate C.:
  1984 *Some Warmer Tone: Alaska Athabaskan Bead Embroidery.* Fairbanks, Alaska: University of Alaska Museum.
  1989 *Northern Athapaskan Art: a Beadwork Tradition.* Seattle: University of Washington Press.
GILBERG, Rolf:
  1986 "A Sauk Chief's Gift: The Complete Costume of Moses Keokuk." *American Indian Art Magazine*, Vol. 12, No. 1: 54–63.
GLENBOW MUSEUM:
  1985 *Metis. A Glenbow Museum Exhibition.* Calgary: Glenbow Museum.
GOGOL, John M.:
  1985 "Columbia River/Plateau Indian Beadwork." *American Indian Basketry and Other Native Arts*, Vol. 5, No. 2: 4–28.
  1990 "The Archetypal Columbia River Plateau Contour Beaded Bag." *Eye of the Angel*. Ed. by David Wooley. Northampton, Massachusetts: White Star Press: 30–34.
GRAND RAPIDS PUBLIC MUSEUM:
  1977 *Beads: Their Use by Upper Great Lakes Indians.* Grand Rapids, Michigan.
HOBBS, Robert:
  1989 "Constancy, Change, and Cultural Interaction in Mesquakie Art." *Art of the Red Earth People: the Mesquakie of Iowa*, ed. by Gaylord Torrence & Robert Hobbs. Seattle: University of Washington Press: 33–51.

JOHNSON, Michael G.:
1965 "Northern Style Fire Bags." *Powwow Trails*, Vol. 2, No. 4: 8–10.
1968a "Northern Woodland Moccasins, Pt. 1." *Powwow Trails*, Vol. 5, No. 1: 4–5,10.
1968b "Northern Woodland Moccasins, Pt. 2." *Powwow Trails*, Vol. 5, No. 2: 16–18.
1968c "Southern Style Floral and Curvilinear Beadwork." *Powwow Trails*, Vol. 5, No. 6: 73–74.
1970 "Notes on the Rymill Collection of Northern Plains Material Culture with Reference to the Plains Cree and Plains Ojibwa." *Powwow Trails*, Vol. 6, No. 10: 185–192.
1972 "Notes on Maritime Algonkin Beadwork." *American Indian Crafts and Culture*, Vol. 6, No. 8: 2–5.
1973a "Floral Beadwork in North America, pt 1." *American Indian Crafts and Culture*, Vol. 7, No. 8: 2–9.
1973b "Floral Beadwork in North America, pt 2." *American Indian Crafts and Culture*, Vol. 7, No. 9: 2–7.
1973c "Floral Beadwork in North America, pt 3." *American Indian Crafts and Culture*, Vol. 7, No. 10: 2–9.
1974a "Decorative Art of the Plains Cree and Their Neighbors, Pt. 1." *American Indian Crafts and Culture*, Vol. 8, No. 4: 2–7,10.
1974b "Decorative Art of the Plains Cree and Their Neighbors, Pt. 2." *American Indian Crafts and Culture*, Vol. 8, No. 5: 2–9.
1974c "Decorative Art of the Plains Cree and Their Neighbors, Pt. 3." *American Indian Crafts and Culture*, Vol. 8, No. 6: 8–11,14–17.
1978 "Material Culture of the Sac & Fox, with Emphasis on the Owen Collection of 'Musquakie' Artifacts." *Whispering Wind*, Vol. 12, No. 3: 4–13.
1990 "Cree Beadwork: a General Discussion." *Whispering Wind*, Vol. 23, No. 1: 4–12.
1991 "Fire Bags of the Canadian Plains." *Whispering Wind*, Vol. 24, No. 5: 4–9.
LANFORD, Benson L.:
1980 "Commentary on Moccasin Analysis." *Moccasin Tracks*, Vol. 6, No. 2: 9–11.
1984 "Winnebago Bandolier Bags." *American Indian Art Magazine*, Vol. 9, No. 3: 30–37.
1986 "Great Lakes Woven Beadwork: an Introduction." *American Indian Art Magazine*, Vol. 11, No. 3: 62–67, 75.
LESSARD, F. Dennis:
1986 "Great Lakes Indian Loom Beadwork." *American Indian Art Magazine*, Vol. 11, No. 3: 54–61, 68–69.

LYFORD, Carrie A.:

1982 *Ojibwa Crafts*. [Reprint of the 1943 edition.] Stevens Point, Wisconsin: Schneider Publ.

OWEN, Mary Alicia:

1902 *Folk-Lore of the Musquakie Indians of North America and Catalogue of Musquakie Beadwork and other Objects in the Collection of the Folk-Lore Society*. Reprint. Nendeln/Liechtenstein: Kraus Reprint. (Publications of the Folk-Lore Society 51.)

POHRT, Richard Jr.:

1990 "Great Lakes Bandolier Bags in the Derby Collection." *Eye of the Angel*. Ed. by David Wooley. Northampton, Massachusetts: White Star Press: 25–27.

SALZER, Robert:

1960a "Forest Potawatomi Men's Apparel." *American Indian Hobbyist*, Vol. 6, No. 5 & 6: 52–58.

1960b "Central Algonkin Beadwork." *American Indian Tradition*. Vol. 7, No. 5: 166–178.

SIMEONE, William E.:

1983 "The Alaskan Athapaskan Chief's Coat." *American Indian Art Magazine*, Vol. 8, No. 2: 64–69.

SMITH, Jerry:

1984 "Ten Garters from the Gilcrease." *Moccasin Tracks*, Vol. 9, No. 9: 8–11.

SPECK, Frank G.:

1982 "The Double-Curve Motive in Northeastern Algonkian Art." *Native North American Art History*. Ed. by Zena P. Mathews & Aldona Jonaitis. Palo Alto, California: 383–428.

THOMPSON, Judy:

1983 "Turn-of-the-Century Metis Decorative Art from the Frederick Bell Collection." *American Indian Art Magazine*, Vol. 8, No. 4: 36–45.

TORRENCE, Gaylord:

1989 "Art of the Mesquakie." *Art of the Red Earth People: the Mesquakie of Iowa*, ed. by Gaylord Torrence & Robert Hobbs. Seattle: University of Washington Press: 3–29.

WARD, John:

1976 "Floral Beadwork." *Indian America*, Vol. 9, No. 3: 14–20.

WHITEFORD, Andrew H.:

1986 "The Origin of Great Lakes Beaded Bandolier Bags." *American Indian Art Magazine*, Vol. 11, No. 3: 32–43.

WOOLEY, David & William T. WATERS:
1988 "Waw-No-She's Dance." *American Indian Art Magazine*, Vol. 14, No. 1: 36–45.
WUDARSKI, Don:
1974 "Iroquois Costume." *Whispering Wind*, Vol. 7, No. 7: 4–12,15.

I. CATALOGUES

ACEVEDO, Alexander:
1983 *Akicita. Early Plains and Woodlands Indian Art from the Collection of Alexander Acevedo.* Los Angeles: Southwest Museum.
COE, Ralph T:
1986 *Lost and Found Traditions: Native American Art 1965-1985.* Seattle: University of Washington Press.
CONN, Richard G.:
1975 *Robes of White Shell and Sunrise: Personal Decorative Arts of the Native American.* Denver: Denver Art Museum.
1979 *Native American Indian Art in the Denver Art Museum.* Seattle: University of Washington Press.
1982 *Circles of the World: Traditional Art of the Plains Indians.* Denver: Denver Art Museum.
1986 *A Persistent Vision: Art of the Reservation Days. The L.D. and Ruth Bax Collection of the Denver Art Museum.* Denver: Denver Art Museum.
EWING, Douglas C.:
1983 *Pleasing the Spirits: a Catalogue of a Collection of American Indian Art.* New York: Ghylen Press.
FEDER, Norman:
1971 *American Indian Art.* New York: Abrams.
HARTMANN, Horst:
1979 *Die Plains- und Prärieindianer Nordamerikas.* 2. ed. Berlin: Museum für Völkerkunde. (Veröffentlichungen des Museums für Völkerkunde, Berlin. N.F. 22)
HAIL, Barbara A.:
1980 *Hau, Kóla! The Plains Indian Collection of the Haffenreffer Museum of Anthropology.* Providence, Rhode Island: Haffenreffer Museum. (Studies in anthropology and material culture. Vol. 3.)
HOLM, Bill:
1983 *The Box of Daylight: Northwest Coast Indian Art.* Seattle: University of Washington Press.

HORSE CAPTURE, George P. & Richard A. POHRT:
1986 *Salish Indian Art: From the J. R. Simplot Collection*. Cody, Wyoming: Buffalo Bill Historical Center.
HORSE CAPTURE, George P. & Terry MELTON:
1989 *The Plateau: The Roger J. Bounds Foundation, Inc. Collection Exhibition*. Cody, Wyoming: Buffalo Bill Historical Center.
MARKOE, Glenn E. (Ed.):
1986 *Vestiges of a Proud Nation: the Ogden B. Read Northern Plains Collection*. Burlington, Vermont: Robert Hull Fleming Museum.
PENNEY, David W. (Ed.):
1992 *Art of the American Indian Frontier: the Chandler-Pohrt Collection*. Seattle: University of Washington Press.
POHRT, Richard A.:
1975 *The American Flag, the American Indian*. Flint, Michigan: Flint Institute of Arts.
WADE, Edwin L., Carol HARALSON & Rennard STRICKLAND:
1983 *As in a Vision: Masterworks of American Indian Art; the Elizabeth Cole Butler Collection at Philbrook Art Center*. Norman, Oklahoma:: University of Oklahoma Press.
WALTERS, Anna Lee:
1989 *The Spirit of Native America: Beauty and Mysticism in American Indian Art*. San Francisco: Chronicle Books.
WALTON, Ann T., John C EWERS & Royal B. HASSRICK:
1985 *After the Buffalo Were Gone: the Louis Warren Hill Sr. Collection of Indian Art*. St. Paul, Minnesota.

K.   MISCELLANEOUS SUBJECTS

BELITZ, Larry:
1979 *Brain-Tanning the Sioux Way*. Pine Ridge Reservation, South Dakota.
BOLZ, Peter:
1987 "Life among the 'Hunkpapas': A Case Study in German Indian Lore." *Indians and Europe: An Interdisciplinary Collection of Essays*. Ed. by Christian F. Feest. Aachen [Germany]: Edition Herodot: 475–490.
HEINBUCH, Jean:
1990 *A Quillwork Companion*. Liberty, Utah: Eagle's View Publ. Co.
MCPHERSON, John:
1987 *Brain Tan Buckskin*. Randolph, Kansas: McPherson.

INDEX

Related Books available directly from the publishers or through your bookstore:

EWERS:	BLACKFEET CRAFTS
LYFORD:	IROQUOIS CRAFTS
LYFORD:	OJIBWA CRAFTS
LYFORD:	QUILL AND BEADWORK OF THE WESTERN SIOUX
SCHNEIDER:	CRAFTS OF THE NORTH AMERICAN INDIANS
UNDERHILL:	PUEBLO CRAFTS

R. SCHNEIDER, PUBLISHERS
312 LINWOOD AVENUE
STEVENS POINT, WI 54481

PHONE: **715/345-7899**
FAX: **715/345-7898**